A Very French Affair

A Very French Affair

A MEMOIR OF ADVENTURE, AMOUR AND A LITTLE MADNESS

MARIA HOYLE

ALLEN&UNWIN
AUCKLAND·SYDNEY·MELBOURNE·LONDON

Some names, places and identifying details have
been changed to protect the identity of the individual.

First published in 2024

Allen & Unwin
Level 2, 10 College Hill, Freemans Bay
Auckland 1011, New Zealand
Phone: (64 9) 377 3800
Email: auckland@allenandunwin.com
Web: www.allenandunwin.co.nz

83 Alexander Street
Crows Nest NSW 2065, Australia
Phone: (61 2) 8425 0100

A catalogue record for this book is available from
the National Library of New Zealand.

ISBN 978 1 991006 63 9

Cover illustration by Sophie Watson
Design by Katrina Duncan
Set in Heldane Text
Printed and bound in Australia by the Opus Group

10 9 8 7 6 5 4 3 2 1

MIX
Paper | Supporting
responsible forestry
FSC® C001695
FSC
www.fsc.org

For Lucy and Susanna

CONTENTS

1

Running Away to the Circus

The air is warm and gentle, and the evening does what long, balmy summer evenings will. It casts a spell. Not that it needs to — this rural French setting is enchanting enough.

We're in the grounds of a manor house — a grand edifice that's peeling and faded but all the more charming for it. A makeshift bar runs across the great entrance to the house, selling wine, beer and plates of cured ham, cheese and bread still warm from the oven. The eccentric outdoor lighting — over-sized modern lampshades on wooden stands placed at intervals on the lawn — casts a glow over the scene.

We sip and we chat, heady on wine and excitement. Dogs stare hopefully at half-empty plates, and children squeal and chase one another among the wooden tables. On this sultry August evening, in a place that is more dimly lit theatre set than garden, it's easy to believe in magic, in ghosts, in a night without end.

The manor house belonged to an old lady who stipulated that, on her death, it must never be sold but used for the public good. Its current residents are a troupe of actors who, in exchange for a peppercorn rent, perform shows throughout summer. In a yurt in the next field a 'circus' is to take place. Not a traditional circus but — it turns out — a theatre of the mind, where a simple trio of performers fires up our dormant imaginations, and we are all six years old again. On a tiny wooden stage, in the middle of a field, in the rural depths of France, I am transported. But then I already was.

I am living an existence I could barely have dreamed of five months ago. Back then, I was content enough with my life in Auckland. Content but also exhausted from surviving in an expensive city. It was a circus of sorts, and I was the resident juggler. *How*, I would think to myself, *did I get to 63 and still find myself renting, working full-time, yet struggling to make ends meet?* I was immensely grateful for my amazing daughters and friends. I was fully aware that my humdrum routine of Wordle, dog walks and early nights with my book was something families in war zones could only dream of. But I was also guiltily pondering: *is this all there is?*

I was online 'dating' — if you can call it that. You know, just in case. The same way some agnostics occasionally go to church. In truth I didn't really see the point anymore. Married for seven years and now divorced, my past was littered with dashed hopes and failed romances . . . ex, ex, ex, ex, ex, ex — like a row of cold kisses.

It's a wonder I was only slightly bruised and not wholly broken. I'd survived narcissists, depressives, control freaks and alcoholics. (Some people were all these things at once.) It's not that I am flawless — heavens no. But I was spectacularly gifted at choosing men who'd flatter the bejesus out of me then inevitably, some months later, express disappointment that I wasn't quite what they signed up for. In other words, that the five-foot package of positivity and delight they first encountered was showing herself to be something quite other — a woman with emotions, scars and needs. That regrettably, because of this, I wasn't a fit for the role they'd had in mind. Consequently, going forwards, they felt cheerful and optimistic about the viability of their personal business without me.

My latest round of online dating only confirmed my worst suspicions. Every snapper-holding, singlet-wearing, Harley-straddling male deepened my despair. Every page of ghastly misspellings and arrogant list of deal-breakers (right up there 'must be drama-free') made my heart sink a little further.

And then I met Alistair.

———

We messaged each other intermittently, with weeks of silence in between. Then one night he left me a voicemail — and that was it. Some people have a thing about teeth, others hands, hair or a way of walking. For me it's voices. Alistair's was an exceptionally pleasant baritone — smooth and playful.

I also liked his approach to life, especially now that we had a lot less of it ahead. Alistair had an explorer's spirit. He wanted to roam and discover — both geographically and in every other sense. He talked about Buddhism and spiritual growth, about travelling and trying new things. He exuded curiosity and dynamism, and I felt that in his company I could expand, not shrivel, as I aged.

He invited me to visit him in Nelson, in the South Island of New Zealand, where he was living until his move to France later in the year. He'd been in New Zealand for fifteen years but now his Irish–English roots beckoned and he was ready to go back to the northern hemisphere. 'I own a mill by a river in France,' he told me. 'Of course you do,' I said. Then I realised he meant it.

His return had been delayed because of Covid travel restrictions and he was eager to be reunited with this 'truly special, magical' place. Alistair told me all this straight away, so I knew it would be an extremely brief liaison. But I still had to go and meet him. Because, well, live for the moment, right? Besides, he fascinated me.

The two weekends we spent together were idyllic. E-bike rides, long lunches, afternoons lying on the grass down by the stream on his property, so much laughing and talking. But when he said 'Why don't you come to France too?' it seemed insane. Nuts. Bonkers. People did that in romcoms. People who looked like Julia Roberts and Marion Cotillard did that. Not your average copywriter nearing retirement. Besides, the romantic prognosis wasn't great. I was easily triggered, way too sensitive for my own good and terrible at intimacy. Not sex, but real intimacy. By what logic, then, did this have a chance of succeeding?

Yet what seemed more lunatic was the notion of spending my remaining healthy years in exactly the same way I had been doing for decades. Doing the nine-to-five grind, always short of money, living in the exact same postcode, with the exact same routine. The more I thought about France, the more sense it made.

I'd grown up in the UK, had family and friends in Europe, spoke French (rustily) and had no house to sell nor swathes of possessions to put in storage.

So I made up my mind to go and began cheerfully (somewhat hysterically) proclaiming to anyone who'd listen, 'Guess what? I'm off to Fraaance!' Without exception they marvelled at my courage, and I basked in their marvelling. Suddenly I wasn't just Maria the short lady with a dog. I was Maria the Brave. Maria with a Plane Ticket to Paris.

Everyone was rooting for me. Even my employer was on board. I went into a Zoom meeting thinking I was about to resign from a job I loved, only to have my manager tell me: 'No, wait. We can make this work. You can't say no to an opportunity like this!' We agreed I'd work part-time, remotely. This type of encouragement — often sprinkled with 'Just do it,' and 'Oh wow, what an opportunity!' — began to dismantle the barriers to making this huge life change.

In my heightened emotional state and believing my own

ridiculous PR, if I'd been asked to pen an official press release on my decision, it would have gone something like this:

'I want to prove that life — even in the third act — can still take surprising turns. That you can look forward to more than cheap bus fares and discounted movie tickets. That love is not only still possible, but it can be the best love you ever had. That maturity doesn't need to be a stagnant pool where expectations go to die. It can be more like the river rushing below the windows of Alistair's beloved mill — ever flowing, swirling, playing and tumbling towards its final destination. That — health allowing — you don't need to do a slow fade but can live each day in glorious technicolour.'

Ha.

———————

You see, it wasn't quite that simple. Just because something makes sense doesn't make it easy. Just because you've styled yourself as a beacon of hope and inspiration for the post-menopausal doesn't mean you're doing mental cartwheels and skipping round your apartment singing *'Je Ne Regrette Rien'*. Not at all.

In the weeks before my departure, I was in such danger of total emotional collapse I ought to have been red-stickered.

I couldn't walk our beloved whippet without getting a knot in my throat when he tilted his beautiful grey head towards me. I couldn't drive anywhere, or pass any park, restaurant, stretch of footpath, or even bus stop without sighing at some lovely memory attached to it. Sculptures I'd previously hated, inconvenient spots where my car had broken down, pretentious cafés I'd scoffed at . . . all were readily scooped up and forgiven. Even traffic cones.

Twenty-three years is a lot of deep roots to pull up. I'd invested years of emotional energy into settling in New Zealand, nurturing friendships, creating a whole new history and narrative. My daughters were just babies in matching gingham outfits when I first landed in Auckland with my Kiwi husband. And now, more than two decades on, Aotearoa was no longer a point on a map; it was in my DNA.

But France . . .

I'd been a Francophile long before I knew what one was. Even the blandness of my first French textbooks, when I was eleven, didn't put me off. 'Marie-Claire is in the garden, Maman is in the kitchen, Papa is at work.' (It *was* the seventies, you understand). Come to think of it, Marie-Claire was never *doing* anything in the garden, just being. So very existentialist.

I didn't get near France until I began studying French at university in my hometown of Manchester. And when I did finally make it — to Paris and later Lyon — I loved it all. The stinky cheeses, the fragrant *boulangeries*, the almost religious reverence for mealtimes, the pungent Gauloises cigarettes, the French way of shrugging and pouting, the *pastis*, the *rillettes* (a very fatty pork spread), the *métro*, the architecture.

That was all a lifetime ago, and I hadn't been to France for well over 25 years. And now here it was, being offered up to me on a plate. Could I really say no?

There was one remaining, and significant, doubt. My daughters. They were my best friends in the world, and leaving seemed like a betrayal. But when I asked them to tell me honestly how they felt, they turned out to be my biggest cheerleaders: 'Come on, Mum! It's an adventure! You can always come back.'

When they saw me still wavering, they hit me with the one thing they knew would seal the deal. The phantom of regret.

'Hey, we don't want you sitting here when you're seventy-three going, "Oh, I wonder how life would have been if I'd gone to France?" We'll never hear the end of it!'

And there it was. That old cliché, 'Life's too short', was no longer just a throwaway remark. It was the final nudge I needed to get on that plane.

2

The Arrival

If my 'emotional reunion' with Alistair were a scene in a movie, it would definitely require a second take. When I arrive at the train station, 50 minutes from my new French home, I am almost incoherent. Two plane marathons, endless interludes of queuing, and a three-hour train ride from Paris have left me worn out, wilted and wondering what's so wrong with dating men, if not in my own postcode, then at least on the same side of the world.

But I am glad to see Alistair, after two months apart. I don't so much embrace him as topple forwards into him like a felled pine tree. He smells nice. His hug is warm and his shirt is cool. I'd forgotten how tall he is.

He leads me to the station car park where his pretty blue Citroën 2CV is waiting and busies himself in the boot, producing first some water and a facecloth. I freshen up in full view of a café table of friends enjoying Wednesday-night beers in the setting sun. 'I thought you hadn't come,' Alistair says as he rummages once more, this time emerging with a basket. 'You were one of the last to get off the train and I thought, "She's changed her mind".' I should have paid more attention to this remark. If I had, I might have avoided a looming mini-drama. More of that later.

In the basket are juicy flat peaches, *camembert*, a fresh *baguette*, fat green tomatoes and slivers of smoked salmon. We set off with the Citroën roof rolled back, gathering speed as we leave the town behind. The *'deux chevaux'* bounces and occasionally rattles, and it's like travelling through the country-side in a giant bread bin. I lift my face to the sky, let the peach juice dribble down my chin and the breeze whip through my hair. We race past fields of sunflowers that are radiant in the golden evening light, then we slow down as we snake through one tiny village after another. The landscape is ridiculously charming: rugged cream stone walls, ivy-clad barns, languid willows and pointy slate-turreted *châteaux* peeping over the horizon like overgrown pencils.

Alistair rests his tanned forearms casually on the wheel, and I try to take it all in. I can't. It's too beautiful, too idyllic. I will have to ingest it one morsel at a time, over the coming days and weeks.

It's dark when we arrive at the *moulin*, but the full moon throws its spotlight on each charming detail. I'm smitten by it all . . . the craggy stone walls, the *moulin*'s shutters, even the old baked-bean can on a stick that warns visitors to steer clear of the ditch by the driveway. Most especially, I am hypnotised by the river, wobbling darkly beyond the trees: a blackcurrant jelly that's not quite set.

But as I later climb the stairs to our bedroom, woozy on tiredness and chilled sparkling *rosé*, I become sharply aware of how far I am from everything I know. There is no sound but the rush of the river. No traffic, no people, not a bark or a siren or a bird call.

If this doesn't work out, I will be adrift like a space traveller cut loose from her shuttle. I try not to think of my daughters back in New Zealand, of the dog wondering why I haven't come home yet, of the 18,000 kilometres between me and everything I have loved for so long. I have to pull the shutters closed on these thoughts . . . otherwise I will drown.

———

Over the next week, I start to become accustomed to my new surroundings. Although 'accustomed' sounds a bit pedestrian. What I am actually doing is slowly waking, rubbing my eyes, and finding the illusion is still there.

I wake daily to what sounds like torrential rain, only to realise I'm in summer now and it's just the rush of the river. As the heavy walnut furniture swims into view when I first open my eyes, I'm reminded with a jolt that this isn't my own home. And as the duvet falls and rises gently next to me, I remember that I'm no longer single but living on the other side of the world with a man I met only months ago.

The sense of unreality is compounded by the shimmering heat and the long, hazy days. To arrive here in the heady midsummer is to step into a beautiful dream halfway through: one that is oscillating, unclear, mysteriously enchanting.

By midday we swelter, our skin glistens and one by one our intentions droop like week-old lettuce. No 'Hmm, shouldn't I be sorting my tax, taking up watercolour painting, signing up for online Pilates?' No, no. It's all out of the question. The heat comes along like a polite but firm butler to remove your shoes, relieve you of your ambitions and plans, plump up your pillows and leave you to get on with it. 'It' being seeking refuge in the river, flopping on the bed like a drowsy cat, or collapsing onto a sunlounger in the shade of the old walnut tree.

The *moulin* sits alongside the beautiful River Vienne, in the French department of the same name. And this tumbling mass of water is a godsend.

When the mercury hits the thirties, I pop on my water shoes and carefully descend the rough stone steps into the cool water. The current tugs at me as it roars past the mill, but it's only kidding. It means no harm. As I make my way further in, it becomes calm again. Even the stones are hospitable, flat and wide like moss-covered ottomans. There's one we call the Jesus Rock because it lies just below the surface so that when someone stands on it, they appear to be walking on water. Another rock is slanted, smooth and large enough for two — that's the sunbathing rock.

The *moulin* itself is enchanting — a three-storey turret of cream and brown stone with bright blue wooden shutters and walls that are solid as eternity. A working flour mill for almost two centuries, it was turned into a rudimentary dwelling some fifty years ago. The first floor is our living and kitchen space, the upstairs the bedrooms. The millstones have retired — one to a life as a picnic table right outside the front door. The other has given itself up to being a layabout, languishing on the ground floor of the mill — a cool, musty space Alistair now uses as his workshop. This is where we enter our fortress — and when you bolt the great wooden door behind you at night, a great sense of safety and wellbeing descends.

Yet I'm not entirely at ease. There are challenges within and without these metre-thick walls. First, the obvious one: will Alistair and I work out? Was this really the best idea? Out of all the things I forgot to bring to France (unbelievably, these include swimming togs), my relationship baggage wasn't one of them. And in all the books I've read on how to win at romance (and I've chewed through a few) I don't ever recall 'move to France' being a tried-and-tested formula for success. Plus Alistair and I didn't even *date*. We totally skipped the 'movies, dinners, walks, getting to know you' stage and went straight to moving in together. *In a foreign country*. Even the most sadistic reality show creators couldn't have dreamed this up.

There's also the challenge of acclimatising to an entirely new culture. And I don't mean the French one. Oh no, that part is relatively simple. I mean how to live in the countryside, when I've always been a cinema, shopping and brunch-with-friends kind of girl. I had pictured the 'French me' frolicking from boulevard to bistro to boutique, with accordionists gaily playing in the background. But the mill is in the heart of 'La France Profonde' — about as depopulated and rustic as you can get. No accordions or happy chatter spilling from cafés. Only the occasional distant bray, the sound of a shotgun from *la chasse* (the hunt), or a church bell perforating the stillness of a sleepy afternoon.

Yes, I should have looked more closely at a map.

The population of our tiny village is just over 400. Standing by the roadside on an average day tells you the inhabitants total roughly two — one of which is an elderly golden retriever called Salsa, regularly to be found waddling nonchalantly down the deserted main thoroughfare.

Salsa and I are already acquainted; she makes it her business to greet everyone. But I'm going to need more than an ailing dog in my social circle. I resolve to make friends. Human ones.

———————

I don't know that much about Alistair, to be honest. He is a whole country to be explored in himself. One thing I soon learn, however, is that he can make anything out of anything and often does. He's practically Leonardo Da Vinci. I can't say for sure if he could cobble together a flying machine or design a self-supporting bridge — but I wouldn't put it past him.

He constantly has projects on the go. Creating a timer device for the old dishwasher so it whirrs into action at midnight on the dot. Converting the 2CV to run on ethanol instead of petrol. And another mysterious endeavour — currently in the conceptual phase — involving the river current and a generator.

Sadly, when it comes to engineering schemes, there is often an environmental cost. In this case, the casualty in our immediate environment is the dining-room table. Yes, all relationships have their conflict zones, and this splendid piece of walnut carpentry has become one of our first.

It's a magnificent specimen that Alistair is rightly proud of. He's extremely protective of it and winces whenever I slide, rather than lift, anything across it. Which is puzzling. Because while he values the table, he doesn't seem to mind that its luxurious grained surface is rarely glimpsed — thanks to the paraphernalia that resides there. We're talking head torches, spanners, tape measures, screws, screwdrivers, documents, plastic folders, books, nuts, bolts and other perplexing bits of plastic and metal. Every now and then I will find a biscuit, a sock or an empty water bottle.

A recent addition is an upturned lampshade that is full to the brim with leads, plugs, a temperature gauge, and a whole range of unidentifiable objects that could be mere junk or critical parts of an ongoing project.

Every night I clear a space at one end of the table so we can eat. It began as me delicately nudging some papers to one side. Now that the items have multiplied, I do it more riot police-style — forcefully pushing back the heaving mass and hardly caring if things get injured in the process.

No wonder da Vinci lived alone.

But hey. It's only a table. And some of Alistair's projects go beyond the merely functional to being sources of great joy — as is the case with the two large, wheeled contraptions that are delivered soon after my arrival. From the living room I hear the metallic sounds of Alistair pottering and tinkering in the workshop below ... and I'm wholly delighted when they emerge as e-mountain bikes some 24 hours later.

To explore the French countryside on these electric marvels is to be *in* it, not just gazing *at* it. It's thrilling — and guaranteed to make you live in the moment. Which is especially *de rigueur* on the gnarliest tracks, if you want to avoid a trip to A&E. The electric factor means we can roam far and wide; but then the thick tyres allow us to go off-piste and a bit crazy.

Our favourite route is along the kilometres of disused railway track near our home, now overgrown with grass and covered with a crisp layer of leaves. It's crunchy and golden, like pedalling over a giant bowl of cornflakes. When we pass the grand cream building that was formerly a railway station, I always find it poignant to think it once connected this little village to the wider world. It's now a private dwelling, and instead of men with whistles and porters lugging trolleys, it's home to a gas barbecue and bits of plastic outdoor furniture.

We also bump along less hospitable terrain where nettles graze your ankles, chunky rocks threaten to de-saddle you, thorny hedges wait gleefully for your next false move — and it's exhilarating. We fly past fields where tractors with seed drills crawl across the land like prehistoric beasts; wobble along behind panicking flocks of sheep; and 'Oooh!' at the glowing embers of red ivy clinging to barn walls. We pass a field of kale and Alistair stops to stuff some in his backpack (we steam it later with lashings of butter and garlic).

Our bikes have throttles (shh, it's not strictly legal). My throttle is a little frisky and when I gingerly attempt to use it, the whole bike bucks like a demented horse. On one occasion we are on a steep, narrow street and I hit the throttle instead of the brake. The bike lurches towards the wall and I go flying, with the heavy metal frame clanging down on top of me. I get up and inspect the damage. My leg is throbbing, my bottom is bruised, but phew — the acrylic nails are intact. Alistair shakes his head.

I clamber back on, determined to show no fear. 'You sure you're okay?' says Alistair, concerned. 'Absolutely!' I assure him. '*Allons-y*, Alonso!'

However, I make the same mistake as we're speeding down a gravel path by a busy road — and only just manage to fling myself to safety on the grass verge. Without a word, Alistair walks over and disconnects the throttle, then gets back on his bike. That is what I call a very sound executive decision.

3

Alistair and the
Giant Misunderstandings

All relationships have their wobbles. There's the honeymoon period, then things start to get real. Alistair and I are nothing if not efficient — not only did we dispense with the dating period, but we also dispensed totally with the honeymoon period, so we hit two biggish road bumps within the first two weeks.

La wobble numéro 1

So how did a man with three citizenships — none of them French — end up in a remote village in deepest France?

Alistair's explanation goes something like this.

'Well, I've always dreamed of living in a mill by a river, and I was on a motorbiking holiday around Europe, and I spotted this ad for a *moulin*, at a ridiculously affordable price. So I came to look — no one was living in it, and I camped in the *moulin* garden' (yes, really) 'to see how I liked the feel of the place, and I fell in love with it. Just the magic of it all . . . the constant rush of the river, the wild beauty of the garden, the old stonework of the *moulin*. Oh, and it didn't hurt that there was a racetrack down the road.'

Here speaks both a poet and a petrolhead.

Alistair is besotted with the rustic life, and I like that about him. I like that someone who'll work himself into ecstasies over satellite internet speed or the pixel density on the latest iPhone will equally pause to appreciate a new bud, or a red squirrel darting across the lawn. However, he's also an unapologetic speed freak, so in this tranquil corner of the land he can have his *gâteau* and eat it. Because nearby, we are 'blessed' with almost four kilometres of motor-racing circuit.

Motorbike racing and rally-car driving have been a big part of Alistair's life, and burning up fuel and rubber is his idea of a splendid day out. He's also a supporter of the Green Party, has set up solar panels in the window to charge our phones, is investigating harnessing the river current to power our electricity, and generally strives to leave the *petite*-est of carbon footprints. So yes, like all of us, he's a mass of contradictions.

I'm introduced to the racetrack even before I meet the neighbours (and it's a toss-up which is the biggest fail).

Having arrived in France late on Monday night, by Wednesday my 'human being to walking dead' ratio has only marginally improved. So I'm not quite prepared for Alistair's plan for the following day.

He has signed up to race his KTM motorbike at an amateur motorcycling track day, and he'd like me to tag along. I had been hoping for a gentler introduction to my new life. You know, things involving picnic blankets, buckets of ice and playfully splashing one another in the river like they do in the movies.

Still, what harm can it do? It's only one day, and I can probably loll around drinking cold beer and reading my book while Alistair and the bike spend some quality time together. Ah, but no. Apparently I'm needed to interpret at the 'safety briefings', something that fills me with apprehension. I don't speak motorbike, not even in English. So my French certainly isn't up to it. I'd envisaged easing myself into the language slowly and gently by, for instance, ordering *apéritifs* or chatting to small children.

On the other hand, immersing myself in an alien world of motorbikes is out-of-my-comfort-zone stuff — and that's got to be good, right? *You wanted adventure*, I tell myself. *And this, my friend, is what adventure looks like.*

In the book I was reading on the plane, *A Short Ride in the Jungle* by the intrepid Antonia Bolingbroke-Kent, she rides her old, tiny motorcycle along the Ho Chi Minh trail through Vietnam, Laos and Cambodia. Every day brings frustration and often fear, but she acknowledges that it is to be 'a journey of small victories'. So while my soon-to-be-faced challenge is nothing compared to this feisty young woman's, it will be a good phrase to remember throughout this French adventure. Indeed, it's a fairly apt summing up of life itself.

The next day, Alistair busies himself downstairs in the workshop-garage and emerges wearing a rather natty orange-and-white leather jumpsuit. I wear my best 'Wheee, this is exciting!' expression because I want to get into the spirit of the thing. He chatters animatedly, even suggesting I interview some of the other competitors 'for your blog'. It's endearing really, how much faith he has in me. I don't have a blog and I certainly don't have the balls to rock up to total strangers to quiz them in a language I barely speak on a subject I know nothing about.

I would point this out but I can see it's futile. Because (and this is an Alistair I am to become familiar with) he is now wholly focused on the mission at hand. His mind is elsewhere — organising, planning — and he is in constant motion, muttering to himself, pacing around finding leather gloves, a helmet to fit me and checking over the bike.

In this state of mind, and in his eagerness to get to the track, Alistair forgets I have never been on a bike before. Bemused by the lack of anything to hold onto, I ask 'Erm, what do I hold onto?' Alistair looks blank. 'Well me, of course.' Why of course.

The other indication that Alistair has forgotten I am a novice is that there are no concessions, speed-wise. We scream along the lanes and, while I can't see on the dial how fast he's going, let's just say I'm expecting an oxygen mask to drop down any minute. I am clinging onto him for dear life, but my hands don't meet around his waist and my grip feels extremely precarious. At one point, we accelerate so suddenly and so hard that I jolt backwards, and my hands almost come free. It's an alarming thought, that it's only my fingertips coming between living-breathing me, and a more roadkill version of myself.

We arrive at the track, and I'm intent on giving Alistair some feedback. Notes, if you will, on his motorcycling performance and what I believe could be improved from a passenger point of view. But I can see it's not the time. He is saying something about a '*boîte*' and how we need to find one, and he's marching towards a shed thing, then we're at a desk signing our names and queuing for something else, and Alistair is talking, and it's hot and there are trailers and bikes and noise everywhere. It's what the French fondly term *le bordel*. I realise I am sounding whiny here, but it's a big leap to go from tranquil riverside utopia to Bedlam Central in one morning.

In jeans and a too thick cotton top, I am sweating and uncomfortable. And that's even before the translating duties. I'm uncomfortable in other ways too — this is *so* not my world. I have no idea what to say or do, or how to behave. I can't even comment on the bikes other than to remark 'such a lovely green' or 'that looks expensive'. As a representative of female-dom, I am doing a great job at reinforcing stereotypes.

A young official at the desk is decidedly coquettish with Alistair, and — kudos to her flirting skills — he seems to have snapped out of his reverie. She's blonde, confident and totally at home in this environment. She *does* speak his language — both bike and English — and knows exactly where to find a *boîte*. I am so tired and dispirited I feel like just exchanging phone numbers for them and booking the first flight back to Auckland.

Ah, but no, Alistair turns and says something to me and indicates that I should follow as he strides *boîte*-wards. A *boîte*, it transpires, is a metal container or private space where you can park your bike and rest between races. Like a movie star's trailer if a movie star's trailer smelled of oil and had nothing in it but helmets, tools and bearded men.

———

The only highlight of the morning is a quick chat with a forty-something woman on a red Ducati, who is standing in the pit lane ready to race. I slink over to her and express my admiration for her bike, and for the very fact she is here in this mostly male world. '*Tu as du courage*,' I say, then tell her I was scared even on the pillion. She laughs. 'Oh God, it's much scarier being on the back than actually piloting. I *hate* being on the back.'

I won't bore you with the rest of the morning.

Suffice to say Alistair does not kill himself (no thanks to my translating) and I learn a list of very useful new words. *Déhancher* (literally, to 'unhip') is what you do when you slide your *fesses* (buttocks) to one side of the bike seat in order to better tackle a corner. Ideally if you can get your *genou* (knee) close to the tarmac as you tackle the bend, all the better. It's what they do in the professional MotoGP races — those young guys have legs of rubber and nerves of steel. Some even get their elbow and shoulder onto the ground as they lean in. Now that's impressive / bonkers.

Then there's the *point de corde* (the apex), and honestly I'm still not even sure what this refers to, but it's something to do with the perfect part of a corner to commence your turn. Erm, that's it. The instructor speaks very, very fast and each time Alistair leans in for his translation, I have nothing. I am, however, becoming fluent in Gallic shrugs. Fortunately Alistair seems to understand much of the briefing anyway, thanks to his experience and some nifty little diagrams up on the whiteboard.

We return home for lunch and Alistair gives me the afternoon off. Which is a nice way of saying I am fired. He roars back to the track but not before telling me the following fun fact. Apparently his ex-partner Sarah was so relaxed riding pillion that she used to nod off to sleep. Well, that's just great.

Feeling like a loser, I am left alone picturing the fabulous time Alistair will be having without me, free to talk engines and hip movements with Mademoiselle Blonde.

I need to do something, pronto, to lift my spirits and regain a sense of self. *A-ha*, I think. It's a beautiful day, and while I daren't attempt to drive yet, I can hop on the lovely green pushbike in the garage. Apparently the famous Sarah used to love a jaunt on the bicycle, and would pedal off happily to the garden centre of an afternoon. I'm going to do just that. A little independent trip, perhaps buy a few seedlings to plant, give Alistair a surprise. Exercise always makes me feel better.

The bike, like everything around here, is *très charmante*. She is a shimmering emerald green with a little wicker basket on the front. I change into shorts, hop onto the *bicyclette* and pedal away, imagining myself in a Stella Artois commercial. There's a slight breeze, the route to the main road is tree-lined and shady and for the first few minutes I'm sailing along, thinking how pleasing it will be to return with a basket full of herbs and plants and possibly a jauntily placed *baguette*.

It's funny how you don't notice gradients till you get on a bike with no gears.

Out in the open sun, on a hill that won't quit, it's torture. I puff my way up one stretch of road, stand up on the pedals to try to make it up the next but simply can't. There is no end in sight — the road is just all uphill from here. I dismount, wishing I'd brought water. I have to get there somehow, even if it means pushing this bastard contraption all the way. Thank God Alistair isn't here to witness this new humiliation.

A motorbike whizzes past and a rider turns to look at me. I scowl back. Not very French of me; round here the accepted form of communication, even with strangers, is a wave and a hearty *'Bonjour!'*

The bike turns and, to my alarm, slows down next to me. Dear God, I do not want to be rescued.

'Hi,' says Alistair, looking amused. 'You okay there?' It's a rhetorical question. 'It's a bit hot in the day to be cycling,' he says kindly. 'Look, why don't you go back home and we can go together in the car?'

My pride is somewhere back on the road, probably with its legs in the air in a ditch, so I nod eagerly. This sounds like a magnificently sane plan.

Turns out Alistair skidded and flew off his bike within minutes of arriving at the track. He's fine but his leg is very bruised and sore, so he decided to call it a day.

Later on, with the heat mounting, we go for a dip in the river. I'm about to sidle up to Alistair to plant a kiss on his stubble, when he says, 'That blonde chick at the desk asked if you were my wife. She was trying to gauge whether I'm available or not.' He is only teasing me, but he's also clearly just a little bit chuffed that someone so young and attractive should pay him attention. I feel a sudden sense of panic.

Now, if at this point you are thinking *Jeez, she's over-sensitive*, you are absolutely right. I mentioned this earlier. I am too sensitive for my own good, and the current situation has stripped me of any resilience whatsoever. I have taken a huge risk here, with Alistair. I have staked everything, every ounce of security I had, to trot across hemispheres to be at his side. But I know very little about him. I know that he prefers *rosé* to red, that he's fond of machinery and fixing things, and that he has a degree in computer science. I know he can't stand ABBA, that he loves mushrooms and can do a spot-on Belfast accent. However, I don't really know whether he's the kind of guy to bolster his 60-something ego by accepting phone numbers from pushy young women.

'Hey,' he says softly, when he sees that I am not laughing. 'It's okay . . . I told her we *were* married! I just thought it was funny, that's all.'

Silence. All I seem to be able to do is stare at the water.

34

'Look, I asked you here because it's *you* I want to spend my life with,' he goes on. 'This is going to work. She wasn't really interested in me and even if she was, it's you that I want.'

He turns me towards him. 'Did you get that? It's you I'm interested in. Nobody else. It's going to be hard, of course it is. We are just getting to know one another. But we are going to make this work. Do you hear me?'

Yes I do.

I am feeling slightly foolish that I made such a big deal of it. I'm not sure what to say. So instead I flick water at him, and then we start to splash each other. Just like they do in the movies.

———————

La wobble numéro 2

I'm not understanding a thing. Yes, language barriers are to be expected — especially since I've only been here a couple of weeks. But Alistair is speaking English.

'Antoine rang and there's a meeting with the mayor on Jacqueline's lawn, and I need to find out about the bread dough, because last year I did the trestle tables . . .'

'Uh?' I look up from the *tranche* of *baguette* which I've been busy slathering in jam like a brickie with his trowel. 'It's nine a.m. on a Saturday and you're telling me there's some kind of committee meeting happening? And why do we — and by that, I mean I — have to go?'

Alistair says more words that make no sense, so I shrug and clatter up the windy wooden staircase to put on some clothes. I'm guessing turning up in your undies is a no-no for committee meetings, no matter how weekend, rustic or French they are.

———————

The heat slides over us like melted butter as we make our way along the river bank to our neighbour Jacqueline's house. The river is clear and conversational, spilling vivaciously over the rocks. A white crane, light as origami, skims the water. At least I think it's a crane. I'm not good on nature. But since flora and fauna are my new neighbours, I'd better get to know them. I make a mental note to find out what a crane looks like, and what he calls himself in French.

In *A Year in Provence*, Peter Mayle writes, 'Neighbours, we have found, take on an importance in the country that they don't begin to have in cities.' Acutely aware of this, and since this is my first encounter with the *'voisins'*, I'm bringing my best Maria forward. She's ready — wide smile, nicely conjugated irregular verbs, eager and poised. Pale blue linen dress — crumpled to convey just the right level of insouciance — heels left at home in favour of easy-breezy white canvas flats, to show I'm as *au fait* with impromptu meetings on lawns as the next person.

Jacqueline lives next door but one, and her lawn slopes nonchalantly down to the water. It's shaded by willows, and the scene when we arrive is all very *Sunday Afternoon on the Island of La Grande Jatte*, except it's Saturday and instead of the bustles and parasols in Seurat's painting there are fifteen or so people in sandals and shorts sitting on randomly positioned dining chairs.

The person I take to be the mayor — solely by virtue of his impressive moustache and the fact he's bent over some kind of ledger — is at a small card table. The rest of the gathering are simply chatting quietly, and some consider me with vague curiosity. I have no idea who or where Jacqueline is. I sit by a grey-haired lady and try to look relaxed, as if attending an al fresco council meeting in a different language on a topic I don't understand is my usual and preferred way of spending a weekend morning.

I smile wanly at my chair neighbour. *'Je suis Maria — je suis la,* um, *l'amie d'Alistair.'*

A flicker of a frown. In strongly Scouse-accented French she replies, 'Oh, where are you staying?'

Clearly the *'amie'* bit didn't quite convey the seriousness of our relationship.

'Avec Alistair, dans le moulin!'

She nods but there it is again. And this time the frown comes with a *soupçon* of an eyebrow raise. She's not the warmest of individuals to begin with, and this hint of disapproval boosts her chill factor by several degrees.

Over the next ten minutes, I have this same conversation with several people. Then it dawns on me. I don't think Alistair has told anyone that I exist. I start to feel unsettled. After all, if a girl is going to skip hemispheres, leave her lovely low-cost rental near the beach, her full-time job, her family, her whippet, her entire life . . . is it too much to ask that the man she's doing it for expresses some excitement to his friends and neighbours? That he offers a little fanfare?

I feel stung. Especially since Alistair used to come here with the aforementioned Sarah, who they all loved. She didn't even speak French but they all embraced her nonetheless. I need to get a grip. This latest bout of insecurity won't do at all.

And then the *pinot* arrives. Sounds harmless enough, does it not? It isn't. *Pinot*, you see, isn't your friendly *pinot noir* or *pinot gris*. This is a local brew of *champagne* and brandy that is both a delight and the enemy of reason.

So when Alistair gestures to me to join him — he's standing in a straggly semicircle of men — I'm filled with indignation. Hurt at not being introduced widely with 'This is the love of my life and she has come to live with me', I ignore him and carry on talking to a lovely English chap next to me who, alarmingly since he's lived here about ten years, speaks no French. I completely shun everyone else at the meeting, mainly because I suddenly feel my stay in France will be very brief.

Later at home, Alistair is clearly displeased with my antisocial behaviour and still simmering resentment. However, we deftly avoid the topic while he fills me in about the meeting. After a three-year hiatus because of Covid, the village *fête* is to be held in a few weeks' time. It's an all-hands-on-deck affair as there is a lot of organisation to do. Now the earlier remarks about dough make sense. The hamlet has a communal bread oven which — back in the day — people could schlepp along to with their gooey lumps of wannabe *baguette* or loaf. It's no longer used except at festival time and, after heating up the oven for three days, the local baker will make bread for several hundred people — both to sell and for the grand communal lunch. Alistair is meant to be helping, but he's not sure in what capacity.

After he's explained all this, we address the events of the morning. Alistair cannot fathom my behaviour. He worries that this is how it is going to be; that he will have to tread on eggshells; he says he can't have someone around who gives in to emotion like that. And then he mentions the D word.

I can't believe that old chestnut, the accusation of 'drama', has arisen so early in our relationship. He had so beautifully sidestepped it during that earlier conversation on racetrack day. He had been sensitive to my sensitivity. But now here it is, and from bitter experience there's usually a swift journey from D to B. Break-up.

Feeling rattled and wanting to make some sense of it all, I head to the river. As I slip into the cool water, I am soothed and forced to dwell in the moment. Wading back to the bank, however, my feet slip and slide on the mossy stones underfoot — as if to remind me I'm on shaky emotional ground. Shivering slightly, I sit on a rock — not yet ready to go inside.

Later, when we have both calmed down, we talk. And I realise something fairly pivotal. Forget French subjunctives and learning the names for the many types of *baguette* (seriously, the *boulangerie* is a minefield). We need to start with the basics, i.e., how to understand each other.

Alistair explains he hadn't told people about me because he was worried I'd change my mind at the last minute. He didn't want to compound the sadness of my no-show with feeling utterly foolish in front of the entire village. Which as I have mentioned isn't that many, even including the animals. But still.

Also he was deeply apprehensive. The 'wonderful Sarah' you see — fit, vivacious, super-active and, like Alistair, full of *joie de vivre* — died of cancer about a year before I met him. She was in her late fifties. He loved her, and the French locals loved her and despite the passing of time and the fact it was perfectly okay for Alistair to meet someone new . . . it worried him. Would they judge him for moving on?

And this really lovely piece of vulnerability and honesty from the man I am just getting to know teaches me two important things: (a) the universe does not revolve around me; (b) never ever accept a glass of *pinot* before 10 a.m.

4

Les Voisins

It's time you met a few neighbours.

Our most important, in many ways, is the river. Because she's always there whenever you need her. Whether it's for an instant cool-down on a hot and humid day, a therapeutic massage in the 'jacuzzi' (where the water spills over the rocks that once formed a weir), or simply lending a sympathetic ear. She's a great listener and has heard many a rant, confession and lament of mine. Cry me a river? Done that.

The Vienne may be a relatively noisy neighbour, but her din is far from unpleasant. She is the first thing we hear in the morning and the last at night — her swirling currents and rushing foam harmonising in a white-noise lullaby. The sound is due to the aforementioned rocks; on walks further along the river bank we marvel at the silence and stillness. However, because these strolls take us along the edge of private gardens, the quiet is invariably shattered by shouts of *'Coucou!'* (Hi!), or *'Bonne soirée!'* from neighbours dining or taking *apéros* (*apéritifs*) outside. No one minds one bit that we pick our way around their garden furniture and over their stone walls. The river is a communal asset, after all.

Our neighbour Gabriel, whose house is also on the water, bathes in it every single day regardless of weather or season. Christine, a diminutive forty-something French potter with curly hair and dimples, comes down to the river at dusk. Living opposite the *moulin* in the tall four-storey house that once belonged to the mill owner, she has no direct access to the water but walks down to the bank to watch the 'fish ballet'. 'The fish, they leap in the air at this time of night. I don't know why they do — jumping for insects maybe? But I love it.'

Others canoe, kayak, fish off the rocks, or swim with their dogs. And with three hydroelectric dams — *'barrages'* — in our nearby village alone, the river isn't just a pretty face but also brings power to her people.

———

I love the river's mood swings. One minute, right before the rocks, she is as calm and unruffled as stretched polythene. The next she's a chaotic mass of curdled foam, all passion and hectic energy as she smashes over the straggly granite barrier. Within seconds order is mostly restored, and she hurries on her way. She has places to be.

We think of this beautiful stretch of water below the mill as 'our river'. Technically Alistair does own this portion, and has even 'gifted' some of the islands (some no more than boulders with weeds) to various friends. One is dedicated to a dear buddy who passed away. Another to his mate Steve. Sarah's is the sunbathing rock. But of course we can no more lay claim to the river than we can to the shimmering blue dragonflies or the otters.

And while the Vienne's incessant chatter lulls us to sleep, we're eavesdropping on a mere snippet of a much lengthier conversation. Stretching 363 kilometres, this major artery of south-western France pulsates through five *départments* (a sub-category of a *région*). Our *départment* of Vienne is one of them. She starts life in the plateau of Millevaches then passes through a multitude of villages and towns — including Limoges (where her water was once used in the making of the famous porcelain), Charente, and L'Isle-Jourdain.

She eventually feeds into the Loire in Candes-Saint-Martin, said to be one of France's most beautiful villages. This seems fitting. If you are going to give up your whole identity upon marriage — as does the Vienne through her union with the great river — you should at least do it in a decent setting.

Fun fact — I used to think *fleuve* and *rivière* were inter-changeable, but no. Which word you use isn't down to choice, but topography. The Vienne is a *rivière* because she flows into another river, whereas the Loire is a *fleuve* as she spills into the sea. *Je vous en prie*. You're welcome.

To live by a river is a wonderful thing, and I never thought I'd hear myself say that. After emigrating to New Zealand, I'd grown so used to being a seaside dweller, to having those vast unpopulated beaches right on my doorstep. In Auckland, the ocean wasn't just a geographical fact, but a forceful presence, a charismatic personality who could take or leave me but who I simply couldn't do without.

Please let me talk about the sea for a moment. Because now I am reminded of it, I have the strongest urge to wade back in.

I've always loved the ocean. Standing with my feet in the water gazing at the horizon, I can't help but sense infinite possibilities. And I have always found the wild, frothing madness of the surf to be both intimidating and invigorating.

I truly believe the sea can heal almost anything, even sadness. Especially sadness.

After one particularly searing relationship break-up, with someone I had met post-marriage, I was invited to a friend's holiday home at Ōrere Point, about an hour south of where I lived. It was an overcast day, but I couldn't wait to get to the beach and hurl myself into the choppy, glacial depths. I'd been crying on and off for days, but as I breaststroked through the churning surf, my tears of self-pity were drowned out by this far greater body of salt water. I swam and I battled the current and I emerged from the ocean not cured, but with a sense that it was all going to be okay. You know, like when you lay out all your jigsaw pieces . . . it's nowhere near a cohesive picture yet, but you know it will be.

Of course there is a scientific explanation for this soothing effect. Ocean swimming helps release feel-good hormones, and the magnesium in the salt water helps to relax muscles and relieve stress. But I still like to think I literally swam through one giant teardrop and made it out the other side.

The sea, to me, is also memory. I'll stand on a shoreline and the past will come swirling around my feet. I'll see my children, glossy with sun lotion and hair like wet seaweed, launching their boogie boards into the waves time and time again — salt-coated, exhilarated. I'll remember a freezing shoreline in Dublin, burying my face into the overcoat of a lover, both of us hungover and knowing it was the end. I'll recall a night in Spain after dinner at a beach restaurant when my late mother — dressed impeccably as always in a silk dress and strings of pearls — threw off her heels, lifted her skirts and splashed into the Mediterranean. I can still see her now, throwing her head back in laughter at my astonishment.

The trouble with memories like this is that you can drown in nostalgia. But the sea, as I have said, won't let you. It keeps you emotionally afloat. I remember another time visiting my mum, realising how few of the old friends remained — the older ones dead and the younger ones gone away. And the grief for everything lost threatened to carry me off on its currents. But when I headed out for an early-morning walk along the sand, before the package tourists had claimed the beach, when the mahogany-skinned fishermen were still attending to their nets, I watched the waves and was reminded of life's unstoppable rhythm. Reminded that all is exactly as it should be. That the tidal metronome will continue to mark time, that people will come and go, that fear will rush in one day, happiness the next. It's just the natural way of things.

So yes. *Saying goodbye to the sea*, I thought, *would be too sad*. And it was. But when we leave behind our friends we don't say 'Well, that's it. I am not going to make any more.' The Vienne is my new friend. She's a different personality, but a friend all the same.

The river is less angry than the sea, but you still have to show respect. The water level by the mill is low, so the chance of drowning is slim. But you must tread carefully, as the stones are slippy and a shin banged against a sharp rock is no fun, I can tell you.

My preferred river attire is an old singlet and a pair of baggy bikini bottoms — or sometimes a T-shirt and shorts. Nakedness would be wonderful but since this is a popular canoeing route, and the canoeists often get stuck on the rocks and linger awhile, I decide best not. It's easy to think you're invisible here, that it's utterly private. But no. Alistair tells me of a former riverside inhabitant who had a thriving cannabis plantation on the little island opposite his home. Seemed safe enough to him. Then one afternoon an off-duty cop came down the river in a kayak with his kids. Long story short, delighted cop, arrested neighbour and as far as I know that was the first and last island cannabis plantation around these parts. (Seems odd to me that a nation which has no problem with a cheeky wine at breakfast has such an issue with cannabis, but hey.)

One afternoon in August, Alistair points out that our local canoe club is running a three-hour excursion at the weekend. The *sortie* includes a guide who will tell us all about the wildlife that inhabits the Vienne. He suggests I go along, given that he'll be busy on a motorcycling trip with some mates from the UK.

I am hesitant. It's not the canoes and the critters that are off-putting, but the notion of diving solo into a group of strangers.

The hardest thing with a new language, I've found, is engaging in banter. Making statements such as 'We live in the old mill by the river' is easy enough. But small talk is an entirely different level of fluency.

Alistair is right though — I can't just sit here watching Netflix while he's away. And after the jaunt down the river I'll be so knowledgeable. I'll be able to point out the window and say annoying things like, 'Ah, look at that young male *Ardea alba* out there (oh, sorry, you know it as an egret), diving into the water for shrimp. No, not that, silly — that's a pigeon.'

Arriving at the canoeing club on the Saturday, I find an assortment of folk — mostly couples or families. A very smiley Mexican lady and her daughter strike up a conversation with me, and I start to relax even more with the arrival of a Dutch couple I vaguely know: Jan, who makes craft beer, and Elsa, who runs horse treks.

Our guide, Philippe, is clad in head-to-toe khaki: long sleeves and long trousers, even on this stifling afternoon. With a large net on a pole in one hand, he looks like he's come as a naturalist to a fancy-dress party. Philippe is a good sort, effervescing with enthusiasm, which is exactly how you want your river guides.

After we've donned life jackets and before we get into the canoes, Philippe lists the wildlife we'll be keeping an eye out for, including the *loutre* (otter); the *castor* (beaver); *libellules* (dragonflies); and *demoiselles* (damselflies).

Everything is making sense apart from the name of one creature that sounds like 'dragondon'. When I inquire what one is, Philippe starts to explain, aided by a sudden outburst of miming from my fellow canoers. One is waving his hand behind his butt to suggest a long tail, another woman is slashing the air with invisible claws, yet another clamping her bottom lip with her top teeth in a display of fangs. Whatever this beast is, I don't want to encounter it. Then suddenly, an epiphany. 'Ah!' I exclaim. 'Now I get it. "Dragon *dents*" — teeth of the dragon! Because it has big fangs.' Everyone erupts into laughter. '*Non*,' says Philippe shaking his head with a smile. '*Ragondin*, not dragondents.' Turns out it is a humble aquatic rodent, the coypu: somewhere between a beaver and a muskrat.

We spend a thoroughly pleasant afternoon, spying no otters or beavers sadly, but when we pull up our canoes at various islands we find an abundance of coypu poo and otter caca. Philippe also points out an impressive piece of trellis work, allegedly the work of beavers, and stumps of wood carved by rodent teeth into perfect pencil points.

My canoe companion is a young man called Luca. He's excited to be coming back from another village for the summer, where he will guide trips like this and spend happy months on the water. 'It's the dream,' he says. Maria, the Mexican lady, has also driven over an hour to be here and I realise how lucky Alistair and I are to have all of this in our own backyard.

Back in the canoes, we shout questions at Philippe or to one another. 'Why is the river so green?' yells someone. I miss much of the reply but the gist is that it's 'good' weed that's nourishing for the wildlife. 'But the locals don't like it and pull it out,' our guide says disapprovingly.

I think it best not to share with the group that tomorrow I will be doing just that, joining a neighbour's working bee to clear their portion of the river. Our immediate *voisins* are sick of all the algae and other plants hampering their enjoyment of the water, so they've invited about forty people to help pluck it out. Afterwards there will be a barbecue on Jacqueline and Gabriel's lawn. I'm all for free food and fraternising with the locals — even if it means indulging in some ecologically questionable activity.

———

I bring up the question the next day, as we're all thigh-deep in water ripping out weed and loading tonnes of the stuff into various canoes, kayaks and paddleboards that people have brought along. 'Pah,' says Fabienne, our immediate neighbour and one of the organisers. 'I have lived by the river for twenty years, and when we first arrived it was like that.' She points to a clear patch of water. 'I'm all for "eco this and eco that", but honestly sometimes these green people exaggerate. If we didn't pull it out, it would choke the river.' Her partner Dom agrees that climate change has introduced this noxious weed to the waterway and that, like climate change, it's not welcome.

I have no idea what to think, but in the name of neighbourly relations and the fact the barbecue smells so good I say, '*Oui*, I understand. And look! There's plenty of weed left anyway!'

The working bee–barbecue is so typical of the French attitude to work-life balance, from what I've seen of it so far. Yes, we spent a few hours slogging away in the river, but we'll be well rewarded with food, drink, music and conversation. The work was a mere prelude, an *entrée* to a feast of a day.

I know few people at the barbecue, but Jacqueline kindly comes to sit by me so I am not alone. It's easy to feel like an outsider; everyone here is either related or has lived in the locality for decades. Fabienne smiles tenderly at the baby she is bottle-feeding — the child of one of her daughter's long-time friends; children are sitting with aunts and uncles; an eight-year-old girl is cuddling her baby sister; old friends are arranging tables and talking easily as old friends do. They have so much shared history, and I am not a part of it. Still, these are excellent hosts and they fuss around me to ensure I feel at home. Who knows . . . maybe one day that shared history of theirs won't matter so much. And shared histories are not only made up of good memories: beneath the surface there may be lingering grudges, misdemeanours not entirely forgiven. I am a clean slate to them. I can be the person I want to be — kind, fun, community-spirited. Someone who will stand shoulder to shoulder with them against a common enemy — even if it is just a few patches of noxious algae.

'Eat, eat!' urges Jacqueline. Formerly vegetarian, I've been literally dining out on the excuse that 'It's not possible to avoid meat over here'. Which is true in rural France, but here there are quinoa salads, roast vegetables, tabouleh, melon, vibrant green salads, tomatoes in oil, olives and golden sticks of crusty *baguette*. As well, of course, as *merguez* — hot spicy sausages — succulent chicken and juicy steaks.

After an hour or so I make my apologies and head back to the mill. They invite me to stay longer, but the introvert in me only has so much conversation capacity. I later watch some of the guests launch their kayaks into the weed-free water, and hear the party's music and laughter late into the afternoon.

———

My second introduction to some of the locals comes one Wednesday evening, at the local campsite. Once a week in summer, the camping ground becomes a social hub for the community, with a cheap set menu on offer.

We cycle the seven minutes to *'le camping'* and sit at one of the many picnic tables under the trees, among families basking in the evening sun. Sunburnt men move slowly like big red crabs, glasses of beer held lovingly between their fleshy pincers. Offspring run gloriously wild — little legs pedalling madly on bikes, scooting along on '*trottinettes*', playing chase or splashing in the pool.

We sip chilled *rosé* from plastic cups, purchased for a song at the *buvette* (kiosk). The *buvette* is run by two ladies I recognise. One of them is a forty-something woman called Carol, who works at the *mairie* (town hall). She is also the postmistress and the librarian. If we ever have a fire, I won't be at all surprised if she also turns out to be the Chief Fire Officer. Or if she's the only person to arrive at the scene, driving the fire truck. For a person with so many responsibilities, Carol is supremely calm and always has time for a little chat.

But then our village, as I have said, isn't exactly a heaving metropolis. You can quite happily vest responsibility for multiple roles in a single individual and they'd probably still have time every day for a three-course lunch and a siesta. There was a time when not just ours, but all the surrounding villages had just one midwife. I once witnessed our friend Antoine talking to a local tradie he didn't know well, asking if he was from round here. 'Yes, I was born here,' the plumber replied. Antoine, also born locally but a good twenty years older, wondered if they'd had the same midwife. He proceeded to ask the man to lift his shirt so they could compare belly buttons. And there they were, like two three-year-olds, gazing at each others' navels with great seriousness. They concluded that the knots looked sufficiently different to cast doubt on the shared midwife theory. I love that with a signature twist of an umbilical cord one woman has put her name to so many local creations.

Ah, but back to the camping ground.

The *buvette* sells wine and beer and an array of soft drinks, but tonight plates of fat, juicy mussels and crisp fries also emerge. The man cooking up the *moules* on a barbecue behind the *buvette* is Marcel, the mayor. To be mayor, it seems, is to be endowed with a flexible schedule, a portable cooking apparatus, a trusty employee called Carol, and a genuine concern that your electorate should be fed and comfortable. (Some months after this, following weeks of rain, Alistair mentions to the mayor that our driveway has become perilously muddy. Our poor Citroën slips and slides on descent to the mill, and one of these days we'll end up in the river. A day later a truck arrives loaded with gravel and fixes the issue. Now that's what I call service.)

Marcel cooks once a week in summer. His repertoire is limited but then he's a mayor, not Gordon Ramsay. We can hardly say 'Call yourself a chef?' when he quite clearly doesn't. One week it's *moules-frites*, the next *saucisses-frites*.

We load up on wine, order our food and Alistair points to a table. 'Here are some people I'd like you to meet.'

The friends are introduced as Brigitte and the aforementioned Antoine, a couple in their sixties who live about an hour away, but spend most of the summer here.

Antoine is like a French-speaking Jack Russell: short, wiry and bristling with energy, even when he's standing still. I like him immediately; he's fully engaged and present when you are talking to him, he has mischievous blue eyes, he smiles a lot, and a joke (or an *apéro*) is never far from his lips.

The French have a reputation for being intolerant if you don't speak their language, but I never find this. Especially not with Antoine — if you say the wrong thing he will look at you with genuine concern, say 'Uh, no, no,' and blink concentratedly as he searches for what you might mean, then excitedly tap you on the arm as he comes up with the *mot juste*. He is always happy to correct you — not in a 'You ignorant clown' kind of way but rather in a 'I love that I am helping you' manner.

Antoine gently puts me right when I describe someone as *débile* (dumb) — the word I want is *faible* (weak). He roars with laughter when Alistair refers to peanuts as an overly literal *noix de singe* (nuts of the monkey), kindly informing him that the word is *cacahouettes*. I am to discover that Antoine knows everyone, will help anyone, and is an absolute treasure.

Brigitte is friendly enough, but a seam of sternness remains. Her welcome is like that of a schoolteacher who feels it's not appropriate to get too chummy with her students. Brigitte is a series of contradictions in a dress. She has warm brown eyes but severe glasses; the deep golden tan of someone who loves nothing better than a book and a sunlounger but silver hair in a neat crop that's all business. I pop her into a file marked 'to be decided'. She and Antoine have been married for 50 years — they tied the knot aged seventeen and nineteen, at the local church. As someone who's rarely stayed in one relationship or one location for more than a year, I can't fathom how that must feel. That depth of history and continuity with one place and one person. It must feel solid. Safe.

Then there is another married couple in their fifties, Annique and Jean. Annique is delightful — petite, lively and eager to chat. Her hair has a sexy Monica Vitti quality. Thick, short and slightly mussed up, it says 'Hey, I used to live in Paris but I've got over myself now.' She and the hair and Jean did live in a Parisian suburb, but moved here some eighteen months ago and 'have never looked back'. Jean has the gentle, avuncular air of a priest (one of the good ones), and spends most of the time talking to Alistair about motorbikes.

Annique wanders off to the loos and when she returns I ask her to point to where they are as I need to go too. '*Là-bas*,' she replies, indicating a row of what look like Victorian seaside changing sheds on the far side of the field. Then she does an extremely amusing low, deep squat with her hands clasped in front to balance her. This is to prepare me for what I will find there. Nothing can prepare you, though, not even an excellent mime. These squat loos are a challenge — and clearly conceived for a clientele who have not just downed four tumblers of *rosé*.

We cycle back home, wobbling slightly more than three hours earlier, but with little danger of anything more serious than a collision with a blackberry bush.

5

Language Lessons

'Learning another language is not only learning different words for the same things, but learning another way to think about things.' — FLORA LEWIS

One of the joys of living in a country where the language is not your own is that even the most mundane transactions and interactions are a chance to acquire new snippets of the native tongue. Every single day, every single thing — be that a trip to the post office, a phone call, neighbourly chat, hair appointment or piece of admin — is a lesson, an opportunity to learn. It's tangible *progress*. Sometimes the progress is glacial, but it's progress nonetheless.

How often in your native land do you return from the

supermarket with a litre of milk and three fresh pieces of vocabulary? I call that a bargain. Even if you think the avocados are overpriced, or the quality of the potatoes disappointing, you'll come back semantically wealthier. Even if, during the shopping itself, you can't locate the spices aisle, you still get to accost a store worker, lob a few hopeful sounds in their direction and congratulate yourself when the word you drag up from the dusty filing cabinets of your mind — *épices* — turns out to be the correct one.

When it comes to comprehension, I've found not all words are created equal. There are whole bits of sentences you can readily dispense with — while certain players carry a greater weight. Misinterpret those, and you're really down a dead-end *rue*.

One day, for example, we were in our favourite shop — the Boutique d'à Côté. This little artisan produce store is a popular hub for locals on a Saturday morning, but you have to get there early to snap up the more in-demand items, like the free-range eggs. We made sure to be there on the dot of 9 a.m., but were disappointed to find the shelves egg-less. *'Bah oui,'* one of the shop assistants began to explain with a sad shake of the head. *'Il a passé le Renard.'* 'How terrible!' I commiserated. I didn't know Renard, but I wanted to show that the omelette-shaped hole in our lives was nothing compared to the loss of this poor chicken farmer. 'Was he sick?' I asked. The woman looked startled. *'Mais non! Le renard . . . il a mangé les poulets!'* Then it hit me — Renard of course, as well as being a man's name, means 'fox'. And the assistant's rather quaint euphemism — 'the fox

57

passed by' — explained why those particular fowl would not be laying eggs that day, the next week, or ever again.

This kind of misinterpretation is how rumours start. Had we not clarified the situation, we might have passed on the sad news to our neighbours, and before we knew it the whole *hameau* would be alight with talk of the mysterious dead farmer.

And that's the danger with language. Any language. Our narratives should all be treated with a healthy dose of scepticism; facts get twisted, crucial details misunderstood, essential words missed.

One day after I was lamenting the lack of restaurants open in the evening, Alistair told me about the wonderful (and ironically named) Hôtel de la Paix. I'd seen the grand cream brick building slumbering peacefully on the edge of the town square, its shutters closed in what looked like a permanent siesta. It had been out of business for two years, Alistair told me. The Hôtel de La Paix had been a favourite with the locals — great food, genial atmosphere, open all hours. And then sadly the owner had stabbed one of the customers and was now in prison. This is what I firmly believed for months. But when we later mentioned the scandalous tale over lunch to our neighbour Antoine, he frowned and said '*Non*, that is not correct — I not know the 'ole story but he definitely stab no one. Per'aps he 'ave retired.'

So the restaurant owner, far from being guilty, was himself the victim of grievous linguistic harm. Alistair or some English person before him had misunderstood the sequence of events.

Perhaps the actual story was that a salesperson had gone into the Hôtel de la Paix touting his dazzling sets of steak knives, and convinced the exhausted proprietor to go into business with him selling kitchen utensils. Or perhaps the owner had stabbed himself by mistake with a meat cleaver in the kitchen, thrown his hands in the air and declared 'That's it! I have had enough of this crazy *bordel* of a life. It is like prison! I move to Provence!' Who knows? I am only glad that, unlike the poor chickens, the wounded customer is a fiction. And that the hotel owner is not eating diluted onion soup in some grim state institution but more likely than not playing *pétanque* by the Med.

———

Alistair and I have had a fair few disagreements about French — or rather, the boundaries surrounding my role as translator. When I first arrived at the *moulin*, he was so delighted to have an in-house interpreter to help him navigate French life that he would use me at every opportunity. Which in some ways is fair enough. But he'd give me no warning or time to prepare. Little swot that I am, I'd have liked a heads-up so I could look up the words for 'septic tank' or 'slow broadband' or 'unblock the chimney'. But no. Alistair would be in the middle of a heated phone conversation when he'd suddenly and exasperatedly hand the phone to me, with the instruction 'Here, you speak French. Tell them that blah blah . . .' Invariably I'd find myself midway through negotiations about complex insurance claims or boiler parts or — the worst one — playing piggy-in-the-middle in a long-running dispute between Alistair and the gas company. I'd be left mouthing silently like a landed trout, not saying anything but staring wide-eyed and panicked.

But not having the right vocabulary is only one issue. You see, Alistair doesn't just want me to *translate* for him. He wants me to *be* him. 'No, no . . . don't be all nice. Tell them we want it delivered TOMORROW or else they can go to hell and we'll go with another provider!!' 'No, don't apologise to them! Tell them we've had enough and that they are incompetent . . . What did you put the phone down for? I had five more questions!!'

Mon dieu — I have agreed to translate, not have a personality transplant.

——————

Despite some of my translation challenges with Alistair, picking up new foreign words is actually such fun. At first, they are nothing more than random sounds made by other people who might as well be miaowing for all that you understand their noise. Then, over time, you recognise the shapes of the sounds, attach meaning to them and finally, one day, you begin to pick them up and make them your own. A new word popped into your repertoire is a wonderful thing. And the best part is it's not like collecting rare Amazonian butterflies or seventeenth-century toothpicks — it's a collection you can readily add to (and show off) every day.

I have gathered some gems over the years. A long-held favourite is *prestidigitateur*, because of its manic, percussive ra-ta-ta-tat rhythm. Pres-tee-di-gi-ta-*teur*. It's a word in tap shoes that comes skittering into the room then lands 'Oof!' in a heap on the sofa. It means 'magician', for which there is also the French word *magicien*. But why would you settle for a mere three syllables when — with a 'Hey presto!' and a swirl of your cape — you can bust out *prestidigitateur*?!

Another one I love is *crépuscule*, because it's just delicious to wrap your tongue around and sounds exactly as the word for 'twilight' should . . . soft, whispery, delicate. A light creeping towards darkness.

But a new favourite acquisition is *enjoliveur* — because it quite literally means 'the thing that makes pretty'. So much lovelier than its English equivalent, 'hub cap'.

The other joyous thing about learning a new language is that it doesn't just allow you to purchase corn plasters or a train ticket to Lille. It sheds light on a culture. It tells you what matters to people, what makes them tick, both on the macro and micro level.

Take the phrase *bon appétit*. It's one we all know and frequently use in our Anglo-Saxon lives, but we toss it around in a rather cavalier fashion. It's more often than not a light-hearted quip, rather than — as in France — a most sincere wish.

At the doctor's one day, I heard every single patient call out to the nurse or doctor on leaving, '*Bon appétit!*' The clinic was about to close for lunch, and these parting remarks showed a respect for the impending midday meal and a shared relishing of the gastronomic pleasures to come. Because in a land where food is so revered, lunch is a sacred fixture. Perhaps not so much in the cities, but in the countryside everything stops. At noon — if not before — people put aways their tools and stethoscopes, pull down shutters, close shops, and shut down their laptops. I once visited a hair salon that had been recommended to me, a good 45 minutes' drive from our home. (The wonderful Cedric, I was promised, will transform you. The only downside is that you don't have a say. He views himself as an artistic saviour, not a hairdresser. He will survey your untidy mop, assess your facial features, and unilaterally decide how to rescue you from this ongoing tragedy.) We decided to make an outing of it and stopped for lunch at a cute little bistro before my 2 p.m. appointment. Walking into the salon after lunch, we were greeted by Cedric gaily brandishing his scissors. 'Ah, we just saw you in the restaurant!' he beamed. 'The staff and I always have lunch there. It's nice to have an *apéro*, and a few glasses of wine, just to give you that break during the day.' I'm happy to report his snipping was still on point.

For me, however, there is also a frustrating side to speaking a different language. In the early stages at least. And that is a sense of loss, a sense that I no longer have access to a certain part of myself. It's like I'm trying to create something in a workshop but someone has waltzed in and nicked my favourite spanners. I don't have the tools I want at my disposal. Take humour, for instance. Humour is my way of building bridges, breaking the ice with strangers. But in France, my remarks get lost in translation. On the rare occasion when I do assemble the words in time, they are delivered with such lack of confidence and such un-comedic timing that they miss the mark.

Interestingly, Alistair — who speaks less French than I do — is far better at this than I am. One day, in the aforementioned Boutique d'à Côté we were buying eggs (honestly we do have other interests) and Alistair knocked the carton off the counter, smashing two on the floor in the process. Switching to my default people-pleasing mode, I immediately began to profusely apologise for the glutinous puddle, check that no one had been splashed, and mop up the mess. Alistair merely handed over the money for the shopping and quipped, 'Some replacement eggs, perhaps?' Everyone laughed good-heartedly, and took it as the joke it was intended rather than a serious piece of impertinence. These artisan eggs, as I've said, are a precious commodity. 'How do you *do* that?' I asked. 'It's all in the eyebrows,' he replied, twitching them playfully. He's right. I need to get fluent in eyebrow.

————————

The most important thing in communication is to hear what isn't being said. —PETER F. DRUCKER

Speaking of Alistair, here is an example of someone whose language really does tell you a lot about the way his mind works.

I'm learning that if I want to air a grievance, or express an emotion, I have to be extremely specific. In short, I have to speak like an engineer or a computer scientist. Because this is how Alistair interprets the world. It is the language he understands. In the very early days — and I refer you back to those two misunderstandings — Alistair accused me of 'stress testing' (a computer science term) the relationship. In other words, I was manufacturing a crisis to see how much pressure his affection for me could stand. He warned me that this was counterproductive.

In another argument, he cried out in exasperation 'It's Boolean!' That one actually stopped me in my tracks. It was a good choice of word because we had to take time out while he explained this computing term. Turns out it simply means that something can only be true or false. By the time we'd discussed the terminology, we had cooled off and the tiff was forgotten. Science-speak will do that. It's a passion killer.

It's not that Alistair is clinical and unfeeling, not at all. But having trained as a civil engineer as well as in computer science, then spending much of his career project-managing, he needs you to give him components he can work with. Ennui, vague sadness, a sense of restlessness . . . these are simply no good to him. He wants to dismantle the problem, examine its parts, and only then can he find a way to fix it.

On another occasion my heightened emotion leaves him utterly speechless. The ingredients in this particular disagreement are eggs, potatoes and garlic. But first, a little background.

As I've alluded to before, Alistair is utterly competent. It's maddening. He's a skilled driver, experienced motorcycle rider, he can sail, horse-ride, snowboard and ski. Oh, and he's an expert white-water rafter, as I discovered one evening going down the river in a makeshift raft on what was meant to be a fun jaunt. Alistair kept critiquing my technique with the paddle until finally I snapped back 'I KNOW HOW TO ROW!!'

'Maria,' he said, trying to control his mounting frustration. 'Just listen to what I am telling you. I did an advanced white-water rafting course so I know what I am talking about.'

At which point I threw the oar in the river and yelled back, 'Of course you bloody did because you are bloody James Bond!'

You get my point.

When he's not being 007, Alistair can also pull apart a car engine and fix it, mend the plumbing, do the re-wiring, tile the roof and re-calibrate the sound system to perfection.

But back to the eggs, potatoes and garlic.

The kitchen is the one place where I feel I can contribute something. As far as I know, Alistair doesn't have any Michelin stars so finally it's a sphere in which I can relax and create something. I'm not a great cook, but I have kept two children alive for 24 and 26 years respectively, so that counts for something.

On the evening in question I am making a Spanish omelette. Traditionally, a Spanish omelette — or *tortilla* — contains only potatoes, onions and eggs. I'm all for riffing on a recipe, but in this case I like to respect millions of Spanish domestic cooks and chefs before me and stick to what works. Yes, you'll find omelettes purporting to be Spanish that contain all kinds of randomness and honestly, I don't have a problem with people using up their cold peas and bits of ham. However, I like my version to be old-school.

Alistair asks if he can do anything so I reply, 'Yes, please. You can chop some vegetables.' To be fair, this is not a precise instruction. I had meant vegetables to go *with* the tortilla, not in it. He begins frantically chopping garlic, because he likes garlic, then wanders over and holds the chopping board over the pan in which I am frying an onion.

'Where is that going?' I ask, trying to keep things light but with an edge of hostility in my voice that would warn less courageous men to back off. 'In the omelette,' he says in a carefree tone that I'm not sure I like.

'It's not,' I retort. 'This is a Spanish omelette. A Spanish omelette never, ever has garlic in it.'

What ensues is a ten-minute debate in which Alistair accuses me of being a garlic-hating, uptight, recipe-following automaton and I accuse him of being a garlic-dependent, tradition-despising ignoramus.

When we finally come up for air, Alistair pleads, 'Just tell me this. What is so wrong with garlic?'

'It's *NOT* about the garlic!' I snap back. If Alistair were a painting right at this moment, he would be titled *Speechless Man with Knife, Garlic and Chopping Board*. He is standing stock still, and all vocabulary has drained from him. After a full minute he says weakly, 'It isn't about the garlic?'

I sigh, tell him to shove the garlic wherever he wants, and stomp into the living room. How can I explain to him that this isn't about an ingredient, but about a threat to my very sense of self? That the house, the workshop, the garage, the cars . . .

these are all *his* domain and the kitchen is my last refuge. That Spanish omelettes have always been my *thing* — and now he is taking that from me too. I feel disenfranchised, de-aproned and dejected.

Yes, it sounds thoroughly ridiculous even as I note this down. But that's the problem with words.

Perhaps I need to rely on them less. Maybe I need to lean more on the Gallic shrug and the eyebrow raise. And, when in doubt, on complete silence.

———————

It's stickily hot, somewhere in the thirties, and right now I'm more damp dishcloth than human. We've driven for two hours to the home of an English couple who have advertised their Range Rover for sale. Alistair wants something to tow his motorbikes, and this looks like a good deal at around ten-thousand quid — an older model but in seemingly mint condition. I am beginning to realise that when it comes to anything with an engine, Alistair will travel great distances to nail a bargain. To say he's obsessed would be unfair; let's just call it passionate.

I'd love to paint a geographical picture of the trip, the names of the towns and rivers, the churches and bridges of historical interest. But the truth is I have no idea where we are at any given point. I also shamefully don't care — the Citroën Berlingo is air-conditioned, the *croissants* I pick up *en route* are plump and buttery, and the view is delicious. We journey through hamlet after hamlet, each one dreamily alike with their cream and grey stone, dozing town squares, *boulangeries, épiceries*, church spires. We pass blazing sunflower fields, and cars hurtle towards us down scarily tight lanes. These skinny roads never look wide enough for two, yet somehow always are. I swear they are breathing in and out just a little.

On arrival we're greeted by Graham — a rotund, pink-faced seventy-something with a white ponytail and jolly demeanour. A Santa in sandals.

The Range Rover is less welcoming. It's grubby, rusty and won't start. Fair enough, too; it's been sleeping under a tree undisturbed for three years and is understandably curmudgeonly about being woken on such a sweltering afternoon. Alistair lifts the bonnet and pokes around then lies down to peer underneath and is generally never still. I'm amazed at his industriousness in this heat. I loiter by with Graham, a former salesman of IT systems who is doing nothing to try to flog this dead horsepower. He just looks on and shrugs; he's selling on behalf of a friend and is keeping out of it. Graham chats happily about grandkids back in the UK; why there's been little music worth listening to since 1973; and his hope for a storm to euthanise the crumbling roof of the *gîte* next to the house (so insurance can pick up the tab). He's funny and entertaining and I can see how he sold enough IT gear for a comfortable retirement at age 53. That's when he and his wife Sally came here, twenty years ago. He chuckles when I suddenly exclaim, 'Oh wow, that *baguette* on your windowsill has ears!' It's their ginger cat — one of Graham and Sally's twelve felines — stretched out on the narrow ledge, looking for all the world like she just came out of a *boulangerie* oven.

Once Alistair has finished looking at the car which — inexplicably — he has decided to purchase, we sit on the couple's patio at an enormous marble table in the shade, drinking very strong Ricard and water. Sally and Graham are warm and friendly, but here is the strange thing. Neither speaks any French. This strikes me as remarkable. They have been here for two decades, have all the time in the world, are intelligent, and they live in a small village. There's no law that says you have to become part of a community, but that must surely be one the of the joys and main attractions of village life. Plus Graham is immensely genial and a consummate storyteller, so I wonder how such a convivial man bears the isolation from local life. When I ask him, 'Don't you ever feel a little cut off, not speaking the language?' Graham pours more water into his Ricard and shakes his head. 'No, not really. We have English TV, and the family comes out to visit.' I find this sad, not just for Graham and Sally, but for communities like this who have wonderful people in their midst who simply can't or won't integrate. Maybe it's a deep apprehension of trying to learn a language and failing. For someone like Graham, who spins such a great yarn, it may simply seem too great a hill to climb, to get to the point where he can be his entertaining self in French (it doesn't stop Alistair, but then everyone is different). Or perhaps they just want a quiet life.

The cat on the windowsill is now sitting up, and I see how frail and tiny she is — a little old lady in a raggedy orange fur coat.

Sally explains she was a wild kitten who came to their house one day and stayed. 'Then she took off again — and didn't reappear for twelve years. She just walked back into the garden and now lives on that windowsill.' Cats are indeed mysterious. But then again, I reflect, thinking about our hospitable yet insular hosts, so are humans.

6

Les Amis

Life goes on being blissful — and how could it not? We have all the perfect ingredients. Absurdly quaint French villages; king-fishers swooping low across the river; Wedgewood blue skies; deserted roads (two cars in quick succession and it's rush-hour); *bonhomie* at every turn, and of course — sorry to rub your nose in it — all that excellent food and wine. There is really very little to fret over at all.

I'm still working, but putting in a fraction of the time I have for the past four decades. This is relative luxury. My employer back in Auckland is allowing me to work remotely and we've agreed on four hours a day. Sending completed tasks from a laptop in rural France to a series of inboxes in urban New Zealand makes me one of that annoying new breed: The Digital Nomad.

My brother William in London emails me an article in a UK newspaper by a lady professing to belong to this fast-growing itinerant tribe. Her piece about being an older woman in a nomad community of twenty-and-thirty-somethings is funny and well written, but I'm sniffy about it nonetheless. 'Ha, she's only in Italy for a couple of months — that's not being a digital nomad. That's taking your laptop on holiday,' I scoff, feeling vastly superior and more authentically intrepid. *She* didn't throw caution to the wind and dismantle an entire life.

The new working hours are perfect, and my workmates are being insanely accommodating. They schedule meetings with 'the French office' for 7.30 a.m. New Zealand time so I can jump online in my evening — and then apologise to *me* for the inconvenient hour. They make cute little videos for me instead of emails to make our interactions more personal, and start every Zoom call with, 'Nah, forget about work. First tell us all about *you*! Is it fabulous? What are you eating? Oh, your new haircut is so French ...' Huddled in polo necks, with red noses and heat pumps blasting, they ooze generosity of spirit. I love them all so much for it.

One night, Alistair and I promise to go with friends to the fortnightly outdoor performance at the Jolie Rosette, the venue where the circuses are held. If this is La France Profonde, then the Jolie Rosette is its epicentre. It's less venue, rather a collection of fields surrounding an old manor house with giant rusty gates, three kilometres from the nearest village. Cats steal furtively through the long grass, no doubt wishing the theatre-goers would shut up, go home and leave them to their private wilderness. I have a work meeting at nine the same night, and I can't ask for a rain check just so I can keep my date with a bottle of *rosé* and a cheese platter. So I mingle for the pre-show drinks then throw off my heels to dash to the field where the Citroën is parked. I settle into the front seat with my laptop and hot-spot off my phone for the video call. It's getting dark, and the only thing that my Kiwi colleagues can see is me in a red strappy dress, mostly in shadow, the flickering outdoor lighting lending a nightmarish David Lynch quality to the scene. My teammates think this is fantastic. Every time I join the discussion, they listen and nod. But then one of them will start laughing. 'Oh my God, you are literally sitting in a field.'

So yes, the work arrangement suits me fine, and leaves me time to do some writing. I say writing, but it's really more scribbles in a notebook — and only because everyone keeps telling me, 'Oh you should do a blog!' I'm not sure about that, but I do harbour a secret ambition of writing a book. Yes, everyone is writing a book these days, but I've always had this feeling that it wouldn't be a proper use of my time. Kind of 'Who do you think you are?' syndrome. Perhaps it's because I come from Manchester.

Still, I have plenty of encouragement. My friends at work have given me a wonderful *'Bon Voyage'* present — a Moleskine travel diary and a book called *A Waiter in Paris*. It's by a young Englishman who finds himself penniless in France and is forced to find work at a semi-fancy but hugely exploitative restaurant.

If this guy can write an entertaining memoir on three hours sleep a night, Dickensian wages and barely any food, surely my well-fed, pampered self can have a crack at it.

For now, my half-time wage goes a long way. Especially because Alistair is not charging me rent or other expenses. We split the groceries occasionally but that's about it. I mention this because it's to become important in this particular love story. Romance is all well and good, but it's nothing if you can't afford the candles. Financial stability is a much underplayed factor in successful relationships. I'd like to take every fairytale ever written and throw in some personal-finance advice for impressionable young minds: 'Yes, he says he has a castle and will take care of you. But do you have a pension fund, just in case he changes his mind?' — while of course adding in a link to reputable providers. 'Sure, he says your eyes are like oceans he can do backstroke in, but are you putting a little cash aside? You know, just in case he's screwing the lady-in-waiting?'

———————

I used to love that *Times* newspaper column, 'A Life in the Day', where they ask famous people what their daily routine looks like. I was always fascinated by the featured celebrity's work ethic, energy and monastic restraint. Their day often went something like this: 'Get up at five a.m. Do an hour of Alexander technique. Drink a hot water. Go for a jog in Hyde Park. Walk our beautiful saluki, Serafina. Dial into the team in New York/Paris/Tokyo and schedule my day's meetings . . .' and so on and so on. They never seemed to *eat*, and if they did it was a green detox juice and perhaps some steamed sole for dinner with a cheeky glass of Chablis at weekends. Such a packed schedule, so little food. Maybe that's it. Maybe if you want to have the sort of success that makes *Times* readers interested in what you have for breakfast, you can't afford to stop for breakfast.

I'm not famous, but I am going to tell you what my new routine looks like anyway. And it involves a lot more snacking, procrastination and online word puzzles than the above-mentioned example. So here goes:

7 a.m. Get up, make myself strong coffee and a lemon juice and honey for Alistair. Tell Alistair, 'Ooh I wish I could be that healthy. But it's so hard to adopt a new habit.' **7.30 a.m.** Sit at my laptop. Do three Wordles — *The New York Times, La Palabra del Día* (Spanish) and *Le Mot* (French) — managing to be at once time-wasting *and* pretentious. **8 a.m.** Log on to work emails, make a list of what needs addressing urgently. **8.30 a.m.** Head downstairs for breakfast (*baguette*, butter and jam, more coffee). **9 a.m.** Work for an hour. **10 a.m.** Zoom with my daughters. Work until lunchtime (fuelled by fruit, nuts and the occasional strawberry tart). **1 p.m.** Sit outside with my notebook, novel and a plate of *baguette*; sweet, nutty *P'tit Basque* cheese, juicy green tomatoes and olives. (Sometimes we hit a local *auberge* and have a four-course lunch with a 50 centilitre *pichet* (jug) of *rosé*. On those days little happens after 3 p.m. except napping. **2 p.m.** Dip in the river. Sit on a rock, look for the telltale V on the water indicating an otter swimming below and dream about writing a book. **3.pm.** Bike ride. **4.30 p.m.** Grocery shop. **6 p.m.–6.30 p.m.** Bowl of peanuts and a Kir (*crème de cassis* liqueur and white wine. I appear to have no trouble making *this* daily habit stick). **7–7.30 p.m.** Dinner. Either fish/*saucisses*/ steak and salad (with more *baguette*) on the deck overlooking the river, or a neighbour's place for a barbecue, or *moules-frites* at the camping ground, or a meal at the local pizza joint. I was going to write 'cheap and cheerful' pizza. But it's neither. The food is fine but the chef-manager François is a brooding and rather rude 30-something. The story goes (and like I said previously, take this with a big pinch of salt) that he used to own the place with his best buddy but had to sell up when they had a falling out. The impending closure came as a blow to one of the part-time locals, a wealthy Italian who holidays here. So he bought the place (as you do when you want to secure a steady supply of *quattro formaggi*) and persuaded François to stay on as manager. Clearly it's no longer a labour of love for the probably once genial pizza chef. Luckily his sourness doesn't extend to the food.

So this daily routine all sounds idyllic, does it not? Well yes. And no.

Because, you see, I have deep pockets of loneliness. And something I think might be grief. *Well, duh*, you are no doubt thinking. *You yanked yourself away from everything you know, and haven't had time to fill the vacuum with any deep friendships yet.* Yes, I knew this would be hard. But '*This will be hard*' as a thought, and 'This is hard' as a tangible reality, are very different things.

I want to call up my friend Mary in Auckland and have her come over for dinner, watch her unpack her own ingredients (allergies) and drink homemade kombucha while I sip on a cheap red, then curl up on the sofa together with tea and Whittaker's dark mint chocolate and guffaw over episodes of *Black Books*. I am aching to hug the dog, to bury my nose in the soft part under his ears and breathe deep the smell of his fur. I want to go for long walks with my daughters, and laugh until I cry with them. (Note to self: do Alistair and I laugh enough?) I want to organise a catch-up with my longtime pal Becky. We'll sit at a café, where I'll get a half-strength cappuccino and some full-strength Becky advice. Nobody does straight-talking like she does, and she's rehabilitated me after many a crisis. She literally drove 30 minutes to my house one Sunday when I was having a meltdown over too much work and too many chores, arriving with a bucket, mop and cleaning products. She squeezed past me and simply said, 'I'll start in the bathroom.' After a live-in relationship ended and I had to move house just before Christmas, she turned up with a Christmas tree, decorations and several bags of homewares.

There are other friends, too: too many to mention, and I miss them all.

At least they are not dead — just down under. We can still Zoom and WhatsApp. But I need to find friendships here, in 3D. People I can call up for a drink, lunch, a walk. A hug. Alistair can't be my sole support system. That way lies trouble.

Having any sort of longing at all, though, makes me feel guilty. Aren't I living the dream? Isn't it paradise here? For years I have been thinking to myself, *if only life was less stressful, if only I could escape the urban chaos, if only I could be carefree, if only I could live in some heavenly European location*. Well, I have that now. So it's unsettling to realise the dream is lacking. What does it all mean? That I will never be satisfied? That I will always want what is out of reach? Or is it that this is *a* dream, but just not mine: something like a Chanel jacket that I've bought in an op shop knowing everyone else will go, 'Wow — what a find!' only to find myself wondering, is this really my style?

There is another layer of interpretation, one I am trying to suppress. (Get up close because I am not quite ready to say it in big font.) Maybe Alistair and I are not right for one another. Maybe this was all a mistake. Maybe I wouldn't be so lonely if we were laughing more and arguing less.

In the E.M. Forster novel *Howards End* (1910), the protagonist Helen talks about falling in love with a young man even before she has met him. She becomes infatuated with his parents, the Wilcoxes, while staying with them and she wants to remain in their life forever. By the time bachelor Paul arrives home, it's a foregone conclusion:

The truth was that she had fallen in love, not with an individual, but with a family.

Before Paul arrived she had, as it were, been tuned up into his key. The energy of the Wilcoxes had fascinated her, had created new images of beauty in her responsive mind. To be all day with them in the open air, to sleep at night under their roof, had seemed the supreme joy of life, and had led to that abandonment of personality that is a possible prelude to love.

Like Helen, was I so primed for a dream (mine being of enduring love and adventure) that when Alistair came along, I was 'tuned up into his key'? Alistair is attractive in that distinguished silvery way, intelligent, tall and solidly ursine — and when I met him he said all the right things. He flattered me, charmed me and sent me water-mill porn. It was hard to resist. So have I just convinced myself of love? He said he loved me very early on, and I felt it was rude not to reciprocate. Well, you can't just leave someone hanging, can you? And there is no good reason *not* to fall in love. Have I, like Helen, thrown not just caution but my own integrity to the wind in order to secure this dream?

The catch is that it's hard to pinpoint any tangible flaws in the arrangement. We've had arguments, Alistair can be snappy (in turn, he says I 'rage'), but we always make up and acknowledge these are inevitable teething troubles. We cuddle and laugh at the thought that this isn't going to work.

But Alistair's switches in mood do concern me. Sure, I am flawed. And I do get angry. Maybe to compensate for my petite stature, I raise my voice and become intransigent. I've been bossed around by enough men to get stroppy about my boundaries. Alistair says I yell, rant and pace. I don't know about that, but you're left in no doubt that there is an issue. Alistair's moods, on the other hand, are so subtle — like fine rain you can barely see, only feel. He doesn't fill a space with rage, he vacates it. And the effect is huge. He has no idea that he is such a big personality that when he withdraws it leaves a dimly lit space where doubt and fear grow. He is like the sun retreating behind the clouds. One minute you are warm and basking in his light, the next bathed in shadow, shivering slightly.

He's stated his mission is 'making me feel loved, supported and safe', and I think he truly means it. At times I feel all of those things. At others I just feel alone.

It doesn't help that when he is engrossed in a task — either buying electronic parts on his phone, watching a car-repair video, or downstairs in the workshop — he sees and hears nothing except the challenge in front of him. Ask a question and you'll either get no reply, or a mumble.

He has mentioned that he and Sarah used to work well, that they did stuff together. So I really want to show interest but I lose track of which particular scheme he is pursuing. The mass of wires, tools and screws on the bench and dining room table give me no clues. The regular delivery of enormous boxes that have the couriers staggering bow-legged down the garden steps might contain anything. He could be developing a new generation of nuclear weapons for all I know.

As I alluded to before, all narratives have more than one side. And I am aware I am privileged in being able to state my own. So in the interests of fairness, I will say this. I, too, withdraw. I spend hours ensconced in my turret, on the top floor of the *moulin*, typing away on my laptop. Just like Rapunzel, only with shorter hair and a deadline. 'I have to work!' I protest when Alistair says he hasn't seen me all morning. 'When I last came in you were talking to your daughter,' he points out.

This is becoming an increasing source of conflict — each of us blaming the other for not being present. And the more we disagree, the more we retreat to our respective sanctuaries.

But for now I'm not overly worried. We're both invested in this dream and will do whatever it takes to make it work.

———————

The house is Alistair's, the furniture is Alistair's, the complex stereo and TV system that I don't know how to operate is Alistair's, the cars are Alistair's. The routine and daily agenda are largely Alistair's. I came here with nothing, and have little prospect of acquiring much of my own. But one thing I can acquire is friends.

Let's look at my progress so far.

There's the woman in the *boulangerie*. She looks about twenty and I thought she was a student, but it turns out she and her husband own the business. We have a thing between us. Fashion. It all started with me complimenting her dress. (Seriously, every single day she is immaculately turned out, complete with false eyelashes, curling-tong-styled blonde hair and quite the parade of frocks.) 'It's from a new boutique, just opened,' she tells me. This is music to my ears. Call it shallow, but I do miss bricks-and-mortar clothing stores. The nearest are an hour away, and the only local alternatives are the supermarket and the little minimart, which sells kaftan-y dresses and 'quirky' knitwear I am not quite ready for.

She and I exchange laments about the lack of tangible shopping options and being forced to take a stab at correct sizes and fabric quality online. The next time I go in for a *baguette de tradition*, she compliments my earrings. The time after that I admire her bracelet. We take a short break from this mutual fanfest, during which I make do with complimenting the pastries. Then one day I walk in, wearing jeans, a blue singlet and a blue-and-white striped shirt from Zara. She points her finger up and down at me and says, '*Love* your look.'

So this is great, but it means that now I can't even nip out for bread without serious thought about my outfit choices. I have a reputation to maintain. It's a cute little thing we have going, but I doubt the conversation will ever extend much further beyond personal styling and when the next batch of *baguettes* will be ready.

Then there is Danielle. Danielle I met at my first Jolie Rosette, about a week after my arrival. Alistair had taken up his favourite position, elbow on the bar with a beer in hand, chatting to Jan (he of the canoe trip). It was 11 p.m. and about an hour past my bedtime. It's not that Alistair was ignoring me, but after a few beers he has settled in for the night. He tends to become more proficient at banter as the night wears on, whereas I invariably start to fade and fantasise about drinking tea in bed with my book. A French woman in her fifties came up and introduced herself. After a very brief and halting chat during which I made a mental note to again download the French Duolingo app, she asked if we should exchange phone numbers. In my tired haze I wondered if she was hitting on me, because nothing in my verbal communication had hinted that I was promising friend material. But she told me she worked at the retirement home so I concluded she was just a kind soul on the lookout for lonely old ladies.

I took her number then promptly lost it when I changed SIM cards. 'Hold the friendship, caller.'

Another friend-in-the-making is Jen, a British woman who lives nearby. Alistair had befriended Jen and her partner Richard at a local *fête* the previous summer, and when we bumped into them at the Saturday morning market, he was quick to introduce me. 'I think you two will get on well,' he announced to us both. This had the effect on me that it did when I was seven and my mum would foist her friends' daughters on me with the words 'You two should play together.' Forced friendships are rarely a good idea. However, Alistair is right. We all go out for dinner the following Friday, and Jen and I spend a good three hours chatting just to one another. We tumble over words in our rush to declare our shared loves (the word-tumbling could also be the wine): board games, Barbara Kingsolver, retro wallpaper, BBC 'Woman's Hour'. She's adorably eccentric, talks even faster than I do, and is fascinating to me. A historian, she's super-smart and intensely animated — often she stares up into space as she talks, as if she's a butterfly collector trying to net each bright idea before it flutters away. Jen and her partner don't live here, though; they only come out to France for two to three months a year. So while that friendship has definite promise, it's not going to sustain either of us for more than several weeks at a time.

The other friend is Marianne. Alistair has known her and her husband Tony since he first arrived here. At 70 years old, she radiates pure childlike energy. Decidedly more gamine than *vieille dame*, she's usually in shorts, showing off her slim, tanned legs, waving her arms around excitedly and more often than not letting out her trademark soprano peal of laughter.

We were once at a comedy show together where the performers actually came up at the end to thank Marianne for her enthusiasm. It's the first time I've ever heard cast members deliver a review of their audience.

Marianne's close-cropped hair is dyed bright red: 'I do zis myself, I get de scissor, I go tak tak . . . I don't 'ave got the money to go pay someone to do it.' No, really, this is how she speaks. If she were an actor pretending to be French, people would be horrified at the gross caricature. But it's part of the package that makes her so delightful. A former military cook, born and raised in London, Tony does the same in reverse. As broad as his wife is slender, he gruffly manhandles each French vowel like he's slamming meat down onto a chopping board. Imagine Bob Hoskins speaking French with absolutely zero concession to pronunciation. These two are a lifeline for the lost and lonely, as well as a hit with the party animals — they run fundraising nights for the *pétanque* club, they organise croquet days, indoor bowls, fancy-dress parties and integrate nervous newcomers into the community. They are the unofficial ambassadors of their village.

There are two things I personally love about Marianne. First, her tenacity. She had a hard life before she met Tony (they were friends for years first). Following her marriage break-up she brought up her daughter Luna alone. She moved from Paris to their small village, and did every single thing on a shoestring. She walked Luna miles to school each morning, made all their clothes, did all the house repairs, fitted her own insulation, took a part-time job at the school, cooked, grew vegetables, did everything to build a comfortable life for the two of them. And she succeeded.

The second thing I love is her candidness. What is interesting is how she gets away with being so outspoken. Alistair is not an easy man to disagree with, but she tells him exactly what she thinks — and with humour. One day at lunch, she blurts out, 'I am sorry Alistair but I do not like your *moulin*! It is cold. Poor Maria, no wonder she is miserable! One day she will leave you if you do not move to a nice place. Sell zis ancient pile of bricks and buy a nice 'ome with big windows and 'eating!' Clearly, the *moulin* is Alistair's absolute pride and joy. It is his happy, magic place. He waxes lyrical about it on a regular basis, extolling the thickness of the walls; the view out to the stone steps and ivy-bearded barns; the beauty of the river;

the absolute and utter specialness of it all. Marianne has essentially said the equivalent of 'Your child is ugly'. But he just stares open-mouthed and laughs.

So 'Operation Friend-Maker' is looking promising. Sadly, just as I have my enthusiasm nicely fired up, I am forced to leave France.

7

Brexit Stage Left

Throughout the night of the twenty-third and the twenty-fourth of June 2016, good citizens of Britain who should have been slumbering comfortably in their cotton PJs were instead wide awake and feverishly counting slips of paper. The sum total of these electoral officials' calculations was a bombshell.

At the time I was living and working for a magazine company in Auckland and (I'm SO ashamed of this now) hadn't paid much attention to the furore surrounding the Brexit referendum. And when I did, it was to listen to some of the only voices I deem sane in politics — those of the revolutionary left. Ah, that surprised you, didn't it? But yes. Their argument boiled down to 'What has the EU ever done for the person in the street?' They had a point. All over Europe the EU had been hard at it foisting austerity measures on workers.

When a British colleague in the office burst into tears on hearing that Britain had severed its European ties, I thought she was being melodramatic. Turns out she had a point too.

My nonchalance at this seismic event comes back to haunt me now that I wish to remain in France. British passport holders now have three months in which to saunter around *châteaux* or order *pastis* on a Parisian terrace. Then it's '*Au revoir*' — see you in another 90 days.

I'd initially thought this was no big deal. (Do you sense a pattern here?) If my right to stay in France expired at 90 days, I would nip over the southern border and hang out in Barcelona for a couple of weeks, renew my visa online and head back. How I laugh now at that naivety. Because the 90-day rule covers the entire EU. You can't simply bide your time ordering *tapas* in a Catalonian bar. It's back to Britain with you until your three months have lapsed.

To apply for a year-long visa, therefore, I must return to London and get my application processed at the TLS — an agency that deals with the bureaucratic tedium on behalf of the French government.

What is interesting is all the chaos and misinformation surrounding the necessary paperwork. '*Mais non!*' is the general reaction. Because the fallout from Brexit is only just registering in the national psyche, our French friends are shocked that I have to leave the country. Most of the English people they know emigrated or bought homes here before the rupture, so they're used to it being a straightforward and relatively benign procedure.

Marianne insists all I have to do is go to the local *préfecture* (the regional administration office attached to the Ministry of the Interior) to get my '*carte de séjour*' (residence permit). I should chat to a lady called Valérie, she advises. 'She is SO nice; she will 'elp you!' I may be naive, but even I know it can't be that simple. The French are famous for their red tape, a legacy of the Napoleonic period. The diminutive general set in train changes that gave the state strong centralised power and left France trussed in bureaucratic bondage. So it seems implausible that all I have to do is take a couple of *pains au chocolat* to a lady named Valérie and I'm sweet for the next year.

Still, Alistair and I decide to try our luck with the civil servants at the *sous-préfecture* some 30 minutes away. What's this '*sous*' business, I hear you ask? Each administrative *départment* has a *préfecture*. But the departments are divided into *arrondissements*, and these have a sub-prefecture. The one near us is decidedly '*sous*'. It couldn't be more self-effacing if it tried. The entrance is through a side door, the waiting room is tiny, and beyond a glass-windowed counter two men sit at computers in a space of hutch proportions. Their PCs appear to have beamed down from the 1990s, and the area is dimly lit and really quite sad. Yet the chap who comes to the window is chirpiness itself. He, too, is horrified to hear the rumour that I need to leave the country when my 90 days are up. He seems to consider this an affront to his personal standards of hospitality. The man exudes concern, like a party host who's just realised you've been standing there for fifteen minutes and still don't have a glass. '*Mais non*!' He looks over at Alistair and asks if he is my husband. I say no and struggle for the word for 'partner'. 'Concubine,' says Alistair, grinning. 'Well then!' says the man, heartily relieved. For him, the matter is settled. If we're a couple, and Alistair lives here, then it's out of the question that we should be separated. If only it were that simple.

Sadly this affable man has no powers to grant a visa, and suggests we try the *préfecture*.

We pick a day to drive to the *préfecture,* an hour away by car. We have a spring in our step, but then so did Dorothy on her way to meet the wizard.

At the *préfecture* — suitably grandiose unlike its little *sous*-underling — a security guard steps forward to apprehend us before we even get a chance to approach the front door. We tell him our business and he asks us to wait. A few minutes later, a woman appears. She wears stern black-rimmed spectacles, her dark hair up in a tight bun and she carries a clipboard. She's the sort of person you simply can't picture ever being a child; I imagine she came out of the womb a fully-formed civil servant, and that her first words were 'Do you have an appointment?' This is clearly not a Valérie-type situation. This is where it starts to get real.

With the security guard still hovering, she asks us how she can help. 'I'd like to renew my visa — I am a British/New Zealand citizen . . .' She doesn't let me finish. 'No, you must go back to where you came from to apply. To London.'

'But I didn't come from London!' I protest. 'I flew here from New Zealand.'

'Oh, well go back there then,' she says casually. She's really not getting it.

'But I don't live there anymore!'

She starts to look both impatient and confused. 'Where *do* you live?'

'Here! With him!' I say, pointing to Alistair — hoping the concubine thing will move her as it did her *sous-préfecture* colleague. Not a chance.

She looks at Alistair for a moment, as if to say, 'What, you couldn't find anything better than *this* in France?'

Then back at me. 'It makes no difference. You must leave.'

I am getting a strong inkling this 'You must leave business' now also applies to this immediate turf.

I try to explain that I don't have an address anywhere *but* here. That I left it all to be at Alistair's side. I don't know why I am appealing to this woman's romantic sensibilities when there is more warmth coming from the granite façade of the building behind her. I am starting to feel upset and afraid, a child lost in the great mall of life. She peers over her glasses and says sorry in a very un-sorry way. 'This is the way it is now.'

Then she deploys it. The B word. It comes down with a kerthunk, like a government stamp on a document. 'Brexit!' It's uttered almost gleefully, with a tone of 'Well, you should have thought of this before you voted "leave".'

'But I hate Brexit too,' I bleat, a lump forming in my throat.

She's already turning to go.

Alistair and I look at each other, defeated, and with time running out.

————————

I don't like border regulations. They are mean-spirited and petty. True, I am not an African or Syrian refugee being tossed in the ocean in an unseaworthy boat, fearing for my life. I am lucky. I have options. (I have much to say on the refugee score, too. If I had my way, people who are simply trying to build a better life or flee war and persecution wouldn't get shipped off to Rwanda but put up at the Hilton.)

Surely a better system could be conceived. Maybe a test of some sort to judge your commitment to the place. Something not based on how much money you have and where you come from.

I say this partly because of my socialist ideals. But mostly because the mayor (he of the mussels) practically conferred honorary citizenship on me at a recent *fête* when he saw me diving into a bowl of *miget*. This traditional staple consists of cheap red wine, stale bread and sugar. I didn't mean to order it. I was at the bar, hoping Alistair would grab me a chilled *rosé*. Our neighbour Antoine insisted I try the *miget*. 'Don't do it,' warned Alistair.

A large red-faced man at the bar heard this exchange and motioned for me to go over. '*Vas-y*, try mine,' he said with a drunken leer. I recoiled, partly because I didn't know him from Adam and slurping from his bowl seemed neither polite nor hygienic. He was very insistent, as the inebriated often are. He called for a spoon and handed it to me. I scooped up a blob of soggy, wine-infused bread and said, 'Hmmm.' It was meant to be non-committal but Antoine took this as a positive review and ordered me one. Suddenly I was surrounded by locals wanting to see the English woman drink the *miget*. It was strong. It was sickly sweet. It was very bread-y. It was like the evil stepmother of *sangria*, or a trifle that had got in with the wrong crowd.

'What the hell,' I said to myself and kept going, eager to please my audience. Our friend Charlotte, visiting from Tours, hissed at me to stop. 'You will be so sick tomorrow — you never know what *dégueulasse* (revolting) wine they put in there!'

Among the onlookers was Marcel, the mayor; who, Alistair told me later, clapped him on the back and congratulated him on having a partner who so readily embraced the local rustic traditions. 'Honestly, he was ready to grant you citizenship there and then,' said Alistair. Sadly no mayor has that power.

I didn't even get a hangover.

––––––––––

I leave for London at the end of September, to stay at my brother's house while I get the visa sorted. As temporary exiles go, it's extremely pleasant. My brother and sister-in-law Fiona are fun, welcoming, live near a park with deer, and it really is home away from home. They also have an adorable cockapoo, Guinness, and I've been missing dog time. And after all, this is why I yearned to return to Europe. Not just to be nearer to authentic *tapas* and Italian architecture, but also to family.

On the day of the visa appointment, I turn up twenty minutes early to the offices of the TLS in Wandsworth. I am clutching my file of hopeful documents. Among them are a typed statement from Alistair saying he is sponsoring me and that even if I lose my current work he will have my back; two copies of a long, sycophantic letter (Alistair's excellent idea), one in French and one in English, saying how much I love France, the food, the language, the culture and that I intend to write flattering travel articles about the place (true). Also copies of my passport, bank statements, job references, proof of income, police certificate, references from past employers and a whole bunch of other bits and pieces they never asked for.

The queue grows very long, but it's just past 2 p.m. so I am glad I am in first.

Three hours later I get my turn at the kiosk. It turns out everybody had the same time slot — 2 p.m. was simply when they opened the doors.

Once they've checked my paperwork and I've parted with not far short of a hundred quid, I'm shunted into another waiting room for the final stage of the process: the fingerprinting. There are at least 30 people waiting, all staring at the blank wall in front of us like they have lost the will to live, let alone recall why they wanted a visa in the first place. I am so ravenous, I am willing to trade both my citizenships for a chunk of chocolate or a date scone.

To pass the time I engage in chit-chat with the young woman next to me. When I tell her that I haven't had lunch she looks horrified, and in plummy Princess Diana tones exclaims, 'Oh God nooo; would you care for some of my bagel?' I decline. On hearing the young woman tell me she has landed a job in a French ski chalet, two girls on either side of me squeal, with identical Sloane Ranger vowels, 'Oh raahlly? How *funny*! We are doing the chalet season toooo!' So yes, there I am with the young and effervescent Ski Chalet Three, feeling like a stale white-bread sandwich in the middle of a plate of smoked-salmon blinis.

On my way out, with my fingerprinting done, they wave and wish me a hearty 'Good luck!' Bless.

After weeks of waiting, having convinced myself that the French have laughed themselves silly over my grovelling cover letter then stamped my file with a '*Non*!', a registered envelope arrives at my brother's house. It's my passport, and inside is a year-long visa.

8

Autumn

When I arrive back at the *moulin* a week later (visa in hand), the village is wearing its autumn overcoat. Back in London my brother had remarked that he isn't fond of this time of year — 'It's too untidy' — but it looks good on our hamlet. It has a messy, tousled beauty now, leaves coating everything like a fiery mosaic. In the evenings the sky glows red and the river blazes beneath. But here's the issue. Vienne is one of France's least-populated areas (the younger *Viennois* tend to leave the villages and towns to seek work in the bigger centres of Bordeaux to the south or La Rochelle to the west). And while the warm weather had seduced locals onto the streets, to concerts, shows, festivals and outdoor restaurant tables, with autumn they have dissolved back through the walls of their homes like ghosts. Even Salsa the golden retriever's appearances are fewer.

Alistair is doing everything to make me feel at home, comfortable and excited about being here. He's created a cosy nook for me to work where it's warm, in a top-floor bedroom with a window that looks down on my favourite walnut tree and a russet and golden carpet of leaves. If I'm lucky I catch a flash of our resident squirrel's auburn coat as he scrambles over leaves to get home to Madame Squirrel and run through his nut inventory.

Alistair arranges outings with our new friends. We go foraging for glossy *châtaignes* (chestnuts) with Marianne and her husband Tony, plus the aforementioned Charlotte from Tours and her husband Serge. Serge is tall and slim with silver hair in a man-bun, an extremely kind face and a keen, youthful way about him. One of his hobbies is roller-blading so I am surprised to discover that he is 73. Charlotte has enviably thick, grey locks cut into a long bob, and flawless skin. Her fine features, coupled with her way of tipping her head back and placing her hand on her chest when she laughs (which is often) reminds me instantly of Meryl Streep. Serge and Charlotte have been together for 50 years, and are still giggly and playful around one another.

The air is crisp and twigs snap under our feet as we stoop to riffle through the leafy layer, popping our glossy bounty into plastic bags that are soon full. Marianne says she will roast her chestnuts; Charlotte suggests making chestnut jam, which sounds like a faff, but I guess it's one way to while away the cold days. (We end up roasting ours in the oven then devouring them with Brussels sprouts, garlic and *lardons*. Magnificent.)

Afterwards we retreat to a nearby restaurant with a 15 euro set menu that is beautifully cooked and, inevitably, all meat or fish. A fabulous pork terrine to start (with a basket of fluffy white bread); a *ceviche*-style seafood salad; tender beef cheeks in rich red wine sauce with *patates dauphinoises*; a cheese platter; and then a chocolate *pavé* (which literally means paving stone) — a rectangular slab consisting of a firm mousse and a layer of biscuits. It's dense but light, which is a blessing after the hefty four courses we've just stashed away.

It's funny what you remember about conversations. From this two-hour lunch I recall only one remark. Charlotte, saying she has no passport and has no plans to get one. Because, 'Why would I want to travel? Look at this place! France is just perfect.' I can't decide whether this is insular thinking, or the wisest thing I have ever heard.

———————

On rainy afternoons Alistair unfurls great maps and talks me through planned jaunts around Spain because he's not forgotten that European travel was part of his 'Come live with me' pitch. He takes me out to cute family-run bistros and, now that there's a chill in the air, he hauls firewood up two flights of spiral stairs so that it's always cheery of an evening. The hearth — while not quite of *Citizen Kane* proportions — is enormous. When the flames get going in the grate, it's pretty much bonfire night at the *moulin*.

One grey day a pick-up truck arrives, its tray piled high with *cordes de bois*, fresh firewood which is tipped out onto the grass by the front door. Alistair and I begin to stack it by the *moulin* wall. Dark clouds glower over us as we work, a stern reminder not to slacken the pace. We've got a good little rhythm going — me picking the logs from the chaotic jumble and passing them to Alistair, who piles them on top of one another. We finish by covering the stack with sheets of corrugated iron to protect our winter insurance policy from the imminent rain.

It feels good to be doing this physical work. Doing it with Alistair. He teases me that I miss the city life — 'your gyms, your clubs, your cocktail lunches'. Ha, who does he think I am — Carrie Bradshaw? In fact he's wrong. Yes, I do love the buzz of the city, but I also enjoy this kind of simple, therapeutic activity. Out in the fresh air. Doing what people have been doing for centuries, stacking the odds in their favour as the bitterest weather approaches. Up to now I've been mostly existing on the fringes of *moulin* life, contributing the bare minimum. Not through laziness but due to both work and writing demands and a certain lack of confidence. I'm like a fish out of water. I'm not a gardener, a DIY-er or mechanic. In this rural setting I feel pretty much useless, to be frank. Having worked as a copy editor or writer for most of my career, my talents are not exactly transferable to rustic living. Knowing where to plant our courgettes would be of far more use than knowing where to place a semicolon. Still, I can learn.

———————

So this is how we sidle into autumn and winter. On vivid, sun-filled mornings it's easy enough to maintain morale. It's when the clouds roll in and refuse to budge for days, surly visitors who fill your life with negative energy, that I have to be on my guard. If not, homesickness will insinuate itself into my thoughts, like a sneaky autumnal draft through a cracked pane.

Looking back, I can see how my homesickness must have frustrated Alistair. 'This is your home now,' he kept saying, adding, 'yes I own it but I want it to be yours too.' He encourages me to put up my own photos and pictures but there are few walls that can be hammered into. He urges me to 'add your stamp' to the living area, but there's little room for manoeuvre because there's nowhere to put the heavy furniture that came with the mill.

He says I should pick a project of my own — the old barn with a collapsed roof, for example. He wants to turn it into a *gîte* that we can live in when we are too old and creaky to climb the steep and windy wooden staircase. But it needs expensive and extensive repairs first and foremost, and I have no money of my own to fund the restoration. There's the garden, but it's huge and it's hard to know where to begin for a novice gardener. I do, however, pledge to start sowing veges in the spring.

I know this all makes me sound resistant to settling in, ungrateful even. This is certainly how Alistair comes to see it. But it's hard to convey just how lost I still feel at this point. I am in that desolate no man's land — away from those I cherish so dearly, but not yet close enough to anyone here to be able to fill that emotional vacuum.

I am aware I must keep my wits about me, otherwise home-sickness will soon be joined by its evil twin: nostalgia. Whispering maliciously into my ear: 'You were happier then.' 'You had so many friends then.' 'You were safe then.'

It's ridiculous. I came here for adventure, to get out of my comfort zone. I can't be defeated by a few falling leaves and a drop in temperature. So I resolve to try a bit harder, to immerse myself deeper.

———————

Of course the locals haven't really vanished. They're just living differently. 'You have to go and knock on people's doors, or invite them over for a cuppa,' says our Norwegian friend, Inger, over a bowl of her creamy pumpkin soup (with *amaretto* swirled through it — divine) and Swedish meatballs. 'It's how people here get through the colder months.' Inger has made her home here and seems happy enough. But she is only in her forties, and married to a Frenchman with whom she has a three-year-old daughter. Your children *are* your roots, that's the way I see it.

As pursuits go, turning up on your neighbour's doorstep with *croissants* isn't exactly daredevil. But to me it's as scary as free-diving. Something in me rebels at the idea of foisting my company and conversation on people uninvited. So instead I ask a few friends and neighbours over, for Alistair's birthday. It will also be a small way of showing my gratitude, to thank him for all the ways he is trying to help me settle in.

Nervous about preparing dinner for people who are no doubt used to excellent home-cooking, I decide on a 'tapas' evening. It's nice neutral territory. Screw up a *coq au vin* or a *blanquette de veau* and I'll be mortified. But with the Spanish option, I can just say, 'Ah, well this is how they serve it in Galicia.' Many of our guests also know I'm of Latin American descent. While that doesn't qualify me as a *tapas* expert, it does cut me a bit of slack.

The day of the *soirée* I spend hours making Spanish omelettes, pork *albóndigas* (meatballs) in thick tomato sauce, *croquetas* filled with creamy bechamel and *serrano* ham, and later rubbing garlic onto slices of bread and topping them with tomato and anchovies. I've also bought quality *chorizo*, olives and some Manchego cheese. I make a jug of strong red-wine *sangria*, and am altogether satisfied with my efforts.

Alistair, however, is strangely nervous about the gathering. 'I don't know,' he says. 'I always worry, "Will people have a good time?"' This is uncharacteristic of him. He's usually the life and soul, especially after a few *pichets* of wine. I tell him not to worry. 'No, but the French — they do things differently to us,' he says. 'I'm never sure what the protocol is with these things.' He's over-thinking it. There will be plenty of food, rivers of *sangria*, music, and besides, they all know one another. What could go wrong?

Antoine and Brigitte are the first to arrive. They've been to the *moulin* plenty of times, but when they come in they seem a little uneasy. I pour them a drink and offer some of the anchovy *crostini* for them to snack on. Antoine is taken aback. 'What, we eat now?' No, I tell him. Just something to *grignoter* (nibble) while we wait for the others to arrive. He waves his hand. 'No thank you. I wait.'

More people clank up the stairs, bearing expensive wine, chocolates and small cakes. They stand around on the edges of the living room, looking a little lost. It feels like a gallery opening where the crowd is waiting for someone to make a speech rather than an informal birthday party.

The long wooden table is set with crockery, and plates of *tapas*. The guests chat quietly and occasionally glance over at the food. I urge them to grab a plate, try some of the dishes. It's past 8 p.m. and they must be getting peckish. Nobody does. Finally, seeing that someone needs to do something, Brigitte takes control of the situation: '*Et bon . . . à table, non?*', she says, announcing that they should all come and sit down. There is a collective sigh of relief as people sink down gratefully on the dining-room chairs, as if finally given permission to relax.

Alistair had been right; he'd told me, 'The French are funny about just standing around eating,' but I wanted it to be casual. A sit-down affair would unfairly elevate their expectations of the menu. But no. Now they're happily passing plates, laughing loudly, sharing their news, asking what's in the *croquetas* and urging me to text them the recipe. It's like the rather sad, awkward crowd of before was simply the early shift who have been replaced by a different set of people altogether — thoroughly effervescent party animals for whom a plate of *albóndigas* served up in an ancient water mill is their idea of the ultimate night out.

———

French eating protocol is just one of several puzzling phenomena. Another is something Alistair and I call 'The Dark Art of Knowing When Things are Happening and Where'.

There is no local website or *What's On* magazine, no central oracle for social gatherings and public events. There are various Facebook pages for English speakers or inhabitants of certain villages, but it's easy to miss new posts and often these contain scant information. You might be lucky to see a poster on a lamp post or fence, but invariably these shed little light either. Often the venue or date will be missing, or in such small print you can't possibly find it or see it when you drive past. We pick up a flyer in a grocery store that has a picture, in silhouette, of children and cows walking on a hillside, a date, and a price. We show it to the lady at the checkout, who nods, points to the paper and says, 'Yes, look. It's a buffet dinner!' Of course.

Calendar highlights exist in the ether, in the collective consciousness, or are promoted by word of mouth. Many is the time when neighbours will say, 'Oh, you weren't at such-and-such last Saturday.' When we explain that's because we didn't know it was on and ask where they heard about it, the Gallic shrugging starts in earnest. *'Um, bah, je sais pas . . . On a entendu quelque part.'* They just happened to hear somewhere.

There are some permanent fixtures, like the weekly markets and the Wednesday-night campground meals (which we only found out about through a neighbour). Other than that, advertising seems to be written in some kind of code.

The Jolie Rosette, where the circus and other live performances take place, is known by that name to everyone — but on posters it's referred to as La Prade à Moutou (sheep meadow). We have friends who live three minutes from it, have been here for decades, and didn't know it existed. Even Antoine, who is plugged into everything and has lived in the locality all his life, had never been because he thought it was an agricultural event.

Then there's the semi-mythical bread woman. For weeks we have been trying to find out more about a lady who is said to drive through our area delivering fresh bread, but no one appears to be able to tell us which days she comes, or what time. She doesn't beep her horn or announce her presence in any way whatsoever. How on earth she does any trade is anyone's guess, but somehow the locals seem to get their necessary carbs from her when they can't make it to the *boulangerie*.

Maybe that's when I will know that I have made it. That I belong. When I sense that it's time to wander out onto the road and, sure enough, a lady in a van stops and hands me a *baguette*.

––––––––––

One afternoon in November, Alistair calls me to come downstairs. He needs my help with the old carriage.

The old carriage is a decrepit wooden affair that has been sitting under a blue tarpaulin in the barn. It's a uniform beige, cobwebby and dust-covered. It has huge wheels, rudimentary spring suspension, and a wooden seat for two. It must at one time have been hitched to a mule, and used to transport flour from the mill. Like everything here, it is a gentle whisper from the past — a thing not dead but merely sleeping, as if placed under a spell.

I have a dream of cleaning this contraption, painting it and buying a donkey of our own. I will ride into the village, *la petite anglaise excentrique*, climb down and rub the donkey's ears. He will be called Frances.

I recently saw the film *Antoinette dans les Cévennes*, where an infatuated young teacher treks through the beautiful Cévennes national park with a donkey, in pursuit of her married lover who's on holiday with his family. The film had me enraptured. Donkey transport seems to me the most romantic thing on earth.

For now, Alistair wants to move the carriage to the big old barn up the road, which he bought from a neighbour to store his two race cars. We tie bits of wire to the two shafts, and then connect these securely to the ride-on lawn mower, which Alistair will drive. I sit up in the carriage, in a sunhat, and imagine myself holding the donkey's reins, its ears twitching happily in the sun.

Everything starts off fine as we rumble up the incline towards the road. When we get to the steepest part, Alistair wisely tells me to hop down. About ten seconds later, the wire comes loose — first on one side and then the other — and suddenly the carriage starts to roll away from us. 'Grab it!!!' yells Alistair, still sitting on the mower. I don't even have time to stop and (justifiably) say, 'How am I going to intercept a moving carriage twenty times my size and weight?' I just need to do something because it is gathering speed towards the river. I sprint after it down the slope and — by some miracle — manage to grab one of the shafts and push it sufficiently hard sideways that it judders to a stop. Alistair is amazed. He didn't really expect me to halt its trajectory. He comes over, wipes his sweaty hand on his shorts, and gives me a big high-five. I feel like that hopeless seven-year-old kid who's finally won her dad's approval. We secure the wires more tightly then I clamber back on as we head up the gentler section of slope near the road.

It's not exactly the most elegant form of transport. The carriage creaks and lurches from side to side as we wobble over the stony, pot-holed thoroughfare. But sitting up high in my straw hat, with Alistair's smack of approval fresh on my hand, I feel like the Queen of the Vienne.

9

Deuche Courage

I am scared of a small yellow car. There, I said it.

The little pat of butter that is our Citroën 2CV — or 'Deuche' as the model is affectionately known to the French — is supposedly mine. Alistair bought her for me to drive. She's cute as a buttercup, with a retractable roof and big goggle eyes. And she terrifies me.

Which is silly. 2CV stands for *deux chevaux*, i.e. two horses. That's a laughable amount of horsepower.

This fear is now out of all proportion, but it stems from my first lesson in Alistair's own blue version. He ended up shouting and I finished by quivering from lip to toe, getting out and slamming the door shut in the middle of a deserted country lane.

(When we have these mini-spats, I tend to exaggerate their significance. If we were dating in New Zealand, like normal people, a little disagreement would simply seem like teething issues, getting to know one another. No biggie. But here, with Alistair as one of only a few friends and my sole support, the slightest whiff of discord triggers the alarm system in my head. These alarms, by the way, are very loud and operated by personnel who frankly need to get a grip.)

I had higher hopes than this. You see, the 2CV means so much to me already. As I've described, the blue Deuche was there at the train station to transport me to the mill after my grand odyssey across hemispheres. She is my first picturesque memory of this magical place and has become a symbol. Of what, exactly, I am not sure. As a car that makes so much sense here, that utterly belongs, perhaps she's a reflection of my aspiration to fit in. To eventually feel part of this less hurried, more traditional world of village *fêtes* and long lunches with wine at 12.30, of 'popping in' on your neighbours and passing the time of day with total strangers.

Like her new yellow sibling, Alistair's car is exceptionally pretty. She's actually less blue, more a matter of opinion. One minute she's summer sky, the next blue-grey like *quand on a le cafard*. Moody. Often lilac-ish. The kind of colour that sparks debates, speculation about overdue eye-tests, and remarks like, 'So that's mauve, is it? Your behaviour at traffic lights now makes so much sense.'

She has a cream leather roof that rolls back, metal eyelids over her headlights, white wheel trims, and windows that open horizontally like wings. The stripped-back functionality of her frame makes her all the more delightful. It's like travelling in a child's drawing of a car, not an actual piece of engineering. Adorable beyond words.

To drive, she is an absolute bitch.

For starters, she's a left-hander. Which is fair enough. When in France ... But then the gear stick comes out on a stalk, with a golf ball-like globe on the end. It's counter-intuitive. The poking-out-ness of the stalk invites you to shift it to one side to change gear. But what you're actually meant to do is turn it. Look, how can I describe it in words when I can't do it in reality? It's difficult.

During that first driving lesson, I had a sense of foreboding the moment I got behind the wheel. I knew this was not going to go well. The Alistair–Maria dynamic is at its least positive when we are in the car together. Even when I am not crunching gears and doing unspeakable things to clutches, I sense Alistair's disappointment in me. His rally car past has got him accustomed to co-drivers, not passengers. I, on the other hand, like to travel as if I were Grace Kelly in *To Catch a Thief*, staring charmingly into the distance. Or taking photos, fiddling with my phone or any number of things that have nothing to do with co-piloting. Alistair expects me to be useful. He tends to bark instructions and really, that is not what I am for.

So yes. That first attempt at driving the 2CV did not go well.

Alistair sees an eccentric vehicle as a challenge. A thing to be tamed and mastered. Give me a difficult car, however, and all I want is to call an Uber. Or settle for one horse, not two. One with a mane and legs.

But I *have* to learn to drive this car. By getting behind the wheel of a 2CV, I will become that little bit more French. Because the 2CV is a national icon. It's as *français* as Bastille Day, overripe *camembert*, and not wearing a bra. The French love her, and more so because the 2CV is no longer a common sight. People actually stare and wave when we drive past or flash their headlights.

Here's a *petite* history lesson for you.

The first 2CV rolled off the line in 1948, the last one some 50 years later. Once an everyday occurrence, they're now a rarity, especially one in as good a condition as Alistair's (thanks to a lot of hard graft by him).

It was conceived as a car for the people, with the original design brief as follows:

> The car must transport four passengers, consume three litres of petrol every 100 kilometres, be able to carry 50 kilograms of potatoes or a demijohn of wine, have a maximum speed of 60 kilometres per hour, can [sic] be driven by women and on the back seat carry a basket of eggs without breaking them.

Sexist but undeniably charming.

Another fact that makes me love this 'Tin Snail' is that it pissed off the Nazis something rotten. There are several stories about Citroën design chief Pierre-Jules Boulanger and his determination to thwart the enemy during the German occupation of France in World War II.

The story goes that he simply ordered the destruction of around 250 2CV prototypes, and refused to give the plans to the Germans as he didn't want the cars used for military purposes.

But I prefer another version of events (thank you, *Top Gear*), according to which Boulanger played hide-the-Deuche. He walled the little cars in buildings, and concealed them in attics and haylofts so the invaders couldn't get their grubby mitts on them. This epic man also organised a 'go-slow' of production on Citroën trucks for the German military. Brilliantly, he masterminded further sabotage by having the notch on the oil dipstick in the wrong position to ensure engine seizure. His tactics had fascist nostrils quivering with rage and he was branded an 'enemy of the Reich'. Insults don't come much cooler than that.

So the pretty blue and yellow vehicles sitting beneath our windows are so much more than 'just cars'. The 2CV embodies the beloved French principles of liberty, equality and fraternity. Before the arrival of the Deuche, cars had been a costly, elitist affair. She kickstarted a French revolution. Rural communities especially loved her go-anywhere suspension, but she trundled her way into the hearts of the entire nation, giving anyone and everyone the opportunity to affordably nip hither and thither in search of demijohns and adventure.

Knowing how much I love the 2CV, Alistair wanted to find an affordable one for me to potter around in. And he spied what he was looking for — a bright yellow Deuche for sale on Facebook. It looked to be in good condition, and at 5000 euros not a bad price.

I rang the seller and we went to see the car — about an hour away — and what ensued was a long, complex set of negotiations.

Essentially, Alistair was wary of JM, the young vendor. He seemed fine to me, but then I trust everybody. If I found a stranger lurking around the house, unless he was carrying a crow bar and carrying a bag with SWAG written on it, I would probably invite him in for a cup of Earl Grey.

Alistair's suspicion arose from two factors. First, JM only spoke French. Not a crime in itself, especially given that we were in France. But Alistair likes to get *all* the facts of a situation, and here he wasn't getting them. A lot of that was down to my translation. Not wanting to show that I honestly had no idea what the vendor was on about, I gave Alistair the vaguest of summaries, which led him to think the seller was being evasive. It wasn't just 'lost in translation' but 'grossly misrepresented in translation'.

The second factor which, phew, I had no part in, was the absence of a *carte grise*. When you buy a car in France, you have to be physically handed this precious scrap of paper, which is the official vehicle registration document. Our vendor didn't have it — it's with the authorities at the *préfecture*, he told us. He explained why, between drags of his Gauloise, and this time even the original explanation was vague. The signs were not good. We worried that if we paid him for the car, or even left a deposit, without the *carte grise* there was nothing to stop him claiming we stole the vehicle.

But we really wanted her.

After a couple of weeks of phone calls and bargaining, Alistair persuaded JM to bring the car to us and we would pay him then. Only, however, if he managed to produce the elusive *carte grise*, and Alistair remained doubtful on this point.

One dark, rainy and fiercely windy evening, JM arrived with the 2CV on a trailer. He'd had to drive for over an hour, and looked pinched with cold. We invited him up to the *moulin* and I sensed a slight tension in the air. We offered coffee and a glass of madeira, and he gladly accepted.

Alistair's suspicions had started to awaken mine. But now that JM was here — sitting in the soft glow of our lamps, chatting to us about growing up in Corsica and gratefully sipping his hot drink — those doubts subsided. My trust in him became absolute when his phone rang and he said 'Sorry, can I get this? It's my mum'.

'Je serai là dans une heure — t'inquiètes pas, Maman,' he said gently into his mobile.

The phone call ended. 'I live at home and my mother wants to know when I'll be back for dinner. She worries,' he said with an embarrassed laugh.

So not a crook at all. Just somebody's son with a passion for cars, trying to make a living.

A deal was struck and on that bitter winter night, this sunny little car joined our family.

The yellow Deuche has been a good buy. Nothing to fault — which can't be said of me. I am starting to get angry with myself. I feel terribly guilty as she sits there all yellow and innocent. Undriven.

One Monday afternoon, when I have done very little but nap and eat bits of *baguette*, I decide I need a challenge. For days I have been slouching around, rudderless. I'm becoming lazy.

Alistair has a hankering for *patates dauphinoises* for dinner, but we have no potatoes. I volunteer to drive to the supermarket, forgetting that the Citroën Berlingo — which I love to drive — is at the mechanic's. I should explain here that the Berlingo is yet another of Alistair's fleet of vehicles. Yes, he has a problem. And yes, our lawn is starting to look like a car saleyard. He simply can't help himself. But the Berlingo is a handy member of our burgeoning four-wheeled family, being roomier than the 2CVs, more van-like and, importantly for me, automatic.

'Take the yellow car,' says Alistair — a sentence he utters, to no avail, several times a week.

But on this occasion I surprise him with a 'sure'. It's time. If this humble four-wheeler was pivotal to frustrating fascism, surely I can summon up the courage to drive the thing. Plus I remember Alistair saying the 2CV is beloved of 'batty old ladies with eco-militancy running through their veins'. I want to belong to that tribe. If there's a club known for its feisty females and freedom fighters, I want in.

Alistair is kind enough to reverse the car out of the garage and point her in the right direction. I climb in, and he comes to the window to give me a gear-lever refresher course.

I bump off up the driveway, at glacial speed, and I slowly gain confidence with the gears. The steering wheel is wider than I'm used to, and the car's minimalism makes me feel a tad vulnerable. Oh, and the accelerator is on the arthritic side. Yet there's a thrill about travelling in her. Perhaps it's down to what Alistair beautifully describes as her 'ludicrosity'.

If you need practice driving a car, these roads are the place to do it. I hardly encounter another motorist until I enter the town, where the mere presence of other vehicles makes me panic. I stall on a slope, just before turning right into the supermarket, with a car right on my bumper. Channelling some of that indomitable French spirit, I tell myself, 'Well, Monsieur Tailgater, you can wait. No one hurries an icon.' I manage to stay calm and not roll backwards, silently thanking my new yellow friend.

Inside the supermarket, I trot around gathering up potatoes, cream and garlic for the *dauphinoise*. I've never felt Frencher.

Back at the car, the parking space next to me is occupied by an old Renault. An elderly Frenchman with a hangdog face that reminds me of Walter Matthau is in the passenger seat. He points to the 2CV's open roof and chuckles, saying something about *hauteur*. I am not sure I understand, but I need to say something in return. So I offer 'This is my first time out in her!'

'Ah,' he says, nodding. 'So you just passed your test?'

Either his eyes aren't what they were and he thinks I am

seventeen, or he imagines I've been failing driving tests for decades, but I laughingly correct him.

'Erm, no. I mean it's the first time driving the 2CV. *C'est difficile!*' His wife returns and smiles at me and the car. '*Regardez pas*! (Don't watch me!)' I joke as I set off, our speed doing justice to the moniker Tin Snail.

Arriving home, there is a spring in my step. My mood has shifted up a gear.

And yes, I am quite aware that driving into the next village to buy spuds isn't most people's idea of bravery. And it's certainly not on a par with challenging the Gestapo. But I'm pretty damn proud of myself all the same.

10

Winter

Winter draws in and our world becomes smaller. The fire crackling in the hearth; our side-by-side places on the sofa where we huddle together under a woollen blanket; the tiny kitchen with its subdued yellow lighting: these are the hub of our existence. When I am not in residence on the couch, I am inhabiting Middle Earth; from 6 p.m. every evening I perch on an ottoman as close as possible to the blazing logs, a glass of Madeira in one hand, a copy of *The Lord of the Rings* in the other, making slow but steady progress through the pages alongside Frodo, Sam and a bunch of rowdy orcs.

As well as inhabiting the same few square metres, Alistair and I also inhabit the same clothes. I don't mean Alistair wanders about in my lingerie — we're not that deprived of entertainment.

(*I* don't even drift around in *my* lingerie. It's way too chilly for sensuality.) What I mean is that our wardrobe rotation is limited; Alistair lives in a plaid, fleece-lined shirt I bought him from TK Maxx. I live in a Zara rendition of the same shirt, but without the cosy lining. I feel we are morphing into some version of the artwork *American Gothic*. Pale, serious, unworldly. Sartorially unimaginative.

Alistair has paid our talented seamstress neighbour, Carolyn, to make curtains for us out of old quilts he found in the drawer of one of the wardrobes. Everywhere are these phantom threads of former lives: the previous mill inhabitants were two elderly sisters, now dead, and we have inherited much of their linen. All I know of them is that they favoured embroidered tablecloths, colourful towels and sheets verging on cardboard stiffness.

The living room's floor-to-ceiling windows are single-glazed, and the cold waltzes right in and breathes maliciously down our necks. Now, however, the heavy golden and russet drapes have stopped that little game. They really are quite sumptuous. Together with an embossed fabric curtain that covers the entrance to the staircase (the cold wafts up from the first floor), the amber glow of the lamps and the flickering fire, it's like living inside a Renaissance painting.

For days on end I don't venture out. By early December it's below zero, and even going for a run is out of the question. Alistair, ever the practical problem-solver, scurries around feeling the temperature of the walls, checking the indoor and outdoor thermometers, hammering wood to make panels in between the stair railings to keep more of the draughts out. Doing battle with cold currents becomes his full-time obsession.

I follow a Groundhog Day routine. Get up, put on thermals, log on to the computer, make tea, stare at the river and wonder how on earth it was ever warm enough to wade in. I think of home. In New Zealand it will be coming into the prettiest, happiest time of year. I've already enviously looked at social media posts about Labour Day swims — yes, those crazy Kiwis actually make a thing of 'the first swim' in late October. I did it once and nearly froze my ear lobes off.

The pōhutukawa will already be in bloom, their brilliant red flowers heralding long, hot, lazy days. The summer-fair season will have begun: the Festival of Roses in Parnell, the Grey Lynn annual fair, the school jamborees. My daughters and their dad will be planning the Christmas Day picnic; debating whether or not to get the dog some antlers for the Christmas Eve walk up Franklin Road to see the lights; possibly even packing for a quick trip away.

I try not to think about this time last year when I loaded up my old Nissan and the five of us — my girls, the dog and my elder daughter's boyfriend and me — headed excitedly to an old weatherboard house at Piha Beach. It was a hop, skip and a lose-your-jandal from the sand dunes, and the huge windows looked out to Lion Rock. Images now flicker across my mind, a poignant home movie: of orange skies and sunset walks; of board games and laughter; me reading Graham Greene on the bed by the window; a whippet softly snoring at my feet and a great granite lion sleeping in the distance; the bush walk that took us to the very top of Kitekite Falls, where we edged along a narrow shelf of rock to the little natural pool above the roaring cascade — a watery royal box looking out over the green lushness.

Now I am here, in this chilly stone-walled fortress. Whenever I start to feel homesick, I remember that I *chose* this. And as fortresses go, it's a cosy one. I find comfort in the blazing fire, the nightly Madeira and red wine, and hearty *bourguignons*. We are lulled into a winter routine that has no seasons, every day the same. It's like a long-haul flight without end.

Then one day we awake from the spell and remember there is a world beyond these walls. Not just beyond them but only three hours away.

'Let's go to Paris,' says Alistair.

FIVE MONTHS EARLIER...
1 August 2022. Gare Charles de Gaulle, Paris

A woman is walking along a railway platform, illuminated by the pale light that streams in through one of the glass panes high overhead. She appears newly minted and fresh as tooth-paste. In a crisp, blue-and-white striped shirt dress and heels — her expression bright and optimistic — she moves like clear water through the crowds. She is excited to be in Paris, you just know it. So intense is her *joie de vivre*, it really doesn't look like she's just travelled for two days.

That's because she hasn't. That's because that woman isn't me.

I watch her with a flicker of envy as I sit waiting on my fat orange suitcase — sticky, exhausted to the point of delirium after my marathon flight from Auckland, hair clinging to my sweaty brow like Velcro. It's 4.30 local time on an August afternoon, and the air is hot and heavy. It's less like breathing, more like poking your head in the oven to see how your *croissants* are doing.

I have three hours to wait before boarding the train that will whisk me to the local station, where Alistair will meet me.

So tired was I at the Dubai stopover that I tried to exchange my New Zealand dollars for *francs*. '*Francs, francs,*' I kept repeating impatiently, as the man at the currency exchange looked at me quizzically. Then the penny, or rather the *centime*, dropped. I attempted some clunky humour to salvage my dignity. 'Haha, I mean euros . . . sorry, been travelling since the 1970s.'

So yes, I watch the elegant stranger walk by and wish I looked more like her. More archetypally Parisian. Like Coco Chanel, Simone de Beauvoir, or Jane Birkin. The only Parisian female I resemble right now is Picasso's lover Dora Maar — but the way he painted her in his cubist masterpiece *The Weeping Woman*. Deconstructed, desperate and with my eyes on a bit wonky.

———————

. . . and back to now. Gare Montparnasse, Paris.

A woman descends from a train, and her step is as crisp as the cold air. It's minus zero outside. Diminutive and with head held high, she is elegant in a long, emerald green, woollen coat and a circular beige hat shaped like the top of a medicine bottle. She really doesn't look like she has travelled for two days. That's because she hasn't. That's because that woman is me — fresh off the train. And this time with Alistair, not on the way to meet him.

It's many, many years since I was in this amazing city. I mean really *in* it, not just wafting through as I did five months ago, *en route* to the *moulin*.

Paris was disappointing to me, the first time I came here from Manchester aged nineteen to work as an *au pair* in the *banlieue* (suburbs). I was expecting a sort of Parisian theme park, with all the clichés served up instantly: chic women, coiffed poodles, cute antique stores, check table-clothed *bistros*, accordion-playing buskers in berets on street corners (I blame those high-school textbooks). Instead I found grime, urban sprawl, McDonald's, poverty. And dog poo. Most Parisians would not stoop, quite literally, to picking up after their fur babies. It got so bad in the late seventies that then Parisian mayor Jacques Chirac introduced *caninettes*, a fleet of Yamahas (also known as *motocrottes* — poop-scooters) whose riders vacuumed up the canine caca as they went. The initiative was received with mixed results, however, and was disbanded in 2001. Now responsibility rests with dog owners, who face a fine for not picking up.

But then, my nineteen-year-old self saw how Paris reveals her charms slowly and that once you have fallen, there is no turning back. Perhaps it's because I was entering life's summer just as Paris bathed in her own July heat. We were in sync, the city and I.

I'd gaze up at the clear blue sky and mistake it for my own future. There was so much promise in the air.

I spent a lot of time then with my university friend Nicky, who was also in Paris working as a chambermaid: me complaining about spoiled children and her sharing jaw-dropping anecdotes about dirty guests. Yet everything was spellbinding to me: our strolls through the Tuileries gardens; our shoestring meals and only-just-drinkable bottles of wine. I recall the time we sat at a public bench opposite a swanky Saint-Michel restaurant, laying out our *baguette* and *camembert* picnic, and the head waiter, crisp linen over his arm, walked over to open our plonk for us with a corkscrew. There was the July evening I turned round on an escalator heading up to the Place de la Bastille and found I was gazing down at the sad, limp penis of the flasher on the step below me —Nicky and I were barely able to breathe for laughing as we legged it out of there. Then there was the time we cycled through the Bois de Boulogne, and later ate bread and *rillettes* in a cinema on the Champs-Élysées, watching *La Fièvre du Samedi Soir*.

So here we are, 45 years later. I'm almost as poor, just as confused about love, but still as excited to be in Paris.

Alistair and I have only two nights here, one more than Supertramp but fewer than some. Like for example US rock legend Jim Morrison, who arrived in Paris in 1971. He never left, dying the same year aged just 27. He is now eternally checked into that famous hotel of the dead, the Père-Lachaise cemetery, along with a host of fellow celebrity guests like Édith Piaf, Oscar Wilde and Frédéric Chopin.

We stay in a functional but friendly hotel some 35 minutes from Notre-Dame on foot. I don't recall the name, or which street, or which *arrondissement*. But I do recall the distinctive horn-sound of the police sirens, our first meal — steak *frites* and a brandy in the *brasserie* by the hotel — the freezing air pinching our nostrils as we walk double-fast, like characters in an old silent film, to flee the cold. I recall the first glimpse of Notre-Dame in her scaffolding prison as repairs continue post-blaze, a grand old lady bearing her humiliation with poise and grace.

I recall the thrill of stepping inside Shakespeare and Company, the Left Bank bookstore that was first opened in 1951 and has become a literary institution. Writers, artists and intellectuals have been invited to sleep among the shelves on beds that double as benches by day. To date tens of thousands of artists — famous and aspiring — have slumbered among the tomes. The bookstore's founder, American serviceman George Whitman, called these guests Tumbleweeds and described his shop as a 'socialist utopia masquerading as a bookstore'. You can still apply to stay there. In exchange you must simply write your autobiography on one sheet of paper, work in the shop, spend some time on a writing project, and read a book every day. I'd trade the chance of staying at the five-star Hôtel George V on the Champs-Élysées to be a Tumbleweed any day.

Shakespeare and Co is the second incarnation of the store. The original, which opened in 1919 and closed in 1941, was a meeting place for all the anglophone literary greats of the time

— Joyce, Hemingway, Stein, Fitzgerald, Eliot, Pound — as well as for leading French writers.

The new store, which also featured in the film *Midnight in Paris*, has a little café attached. We take refuge in this tiny space, and find three young people chatting to one another behind the counter, none of them apparently interested in serving us. But this is not the stereotypical rudeness of Parisian wait-staff. By the look of them these are fresh Tumbleweeds, and I don't take their indifference as an insult. Instead it amuses me. I conclude that they are so in awe at their own good fortune, they are simply unable to function in any pragmatic capacity.

My next Parisian highlight is the Louvre. Or rather it is meant to be, but we only have a couple of hours to visit and much of the time is taken up with two frustrations. One, the Louvre now uses Nintendos as its audio-guides. I fully accept that this is moving with the times and scores of people appear to be happily plugged into them, looking up at paintings and nodding sagely, clearly getting full artistic support from their little plastic companions. Not me. Not even Alistair, with his degree in computer science. We can't figure out how they work, can't find the exhibits we want, and get mismatched commentary to the artwork in question. In short, we dump the Nintendos back on the desk we'd hired them from (Alistair a tad too loudly and angrily, I feel). We agree to explore the gallery separately and meet up later. I meander around the gallery of antiquities, awed by the red marble walls and soothed and placated by the white marble beauty of the armless *Venus de Milo*.

I meet Alistair at our agreed spot, but then spend a good 35 minutes sitting under the vast glass pyramid ceiling while he paces up and down talking into his mobile. He is doing a deal, purchasing a second-hand Range Rover, and is determined to snaffle this alleged bargain. I'm a little bemused by his priorities — second-hand car deal versus centuries of artistic treasures to gaze upon — but decide to calm the hell down and appreciate the living exhibits, i.e. the gallery visitors. Especially their attire. The puffer jacket appears to be the winter apparel of choice, and while it's practical, it is a little disappointing in this capital of chic.

But then I am wearing the best coat ever. The coat I had to wage a campaign over.

Alistair had suggested that, being in the country now, I should perhaps prioritise function over form when it came to winter-wear. He well-meaningly sent me links to Barbour knock-offs on Ali Express, and I stopped making polite noises of appreciation when he subsequently flicked a few sad anoraks my way for good measure. Clearly we weren't sharing the same vision of wintry me. I was thinking Taylor Swift, cottage-core vibes. Elegance with a nod to rusticity.

In the fashion-magazine world where I once worked, they talk of dresses that can take you from workplace to wine bar, conference call to cocktails. I wanted a coat that would take me from barnyard to *bistro*, from woodland walk to winery. Alistair said that was a lovely idea but also ludicrous. I would not wear a long coat. It was impractical. Which is why, from day one of purchasing my long, woollen, green beauty, I have worn the bejesus out of it. Never has anyone remained so consistently stylish while simultaneously going 'Nah nah na-na-na'. On walks, to the supermarket, in the car, at lunch, on visits to friends, in the garden ... this coat is my QED, my 'I told you so' and is absolutely killing it in the cost-per-wear stakes.

So the Louvre loiterers can keep their sleeping bags with sleeves. I'm out-Parisienning the Parisians.

———————

That night, we eat at an over-priced, rather touristy *brasserie* just opposite Notre-Dame. Not because we are fools, but because we are drawn by the colossal TV that will be screening live the 2022 FIFA World Cup match between Morocco and France. We are trading quality for atmosphere. And boy do we get our atmosphere's worth.

First, the vibe emanating from our wait-person. Tall, handsome, lithe as *fettuccini*, black hair swept back tightly in a bun, he is all sass and grace. It's like being served by a bored ballerina. He manages to remain both disdainful and polite, which is quite the balancing act. His reserve is in contrast to the mayhem all around us, as the room breaks out with whoops, cheers at regular intervals and unadulterated bonkers-ness when France seals the deal with a 2–0 win.

We head outside into the freezing night, scarves around noses, to be greeted by scenes of joyful anarchy. France supporters are everywhere, and cars streaming over the Pont Notre-Dame struggle to advance through the tide of red, white and blue. Fans surround vehicles as they pass, rocking them from side to side but, to my surprise, drivers and passengers alike just shake their heads and laugh. Cops stand by uninterested; they've seen it all before.

———————

Alistair has decided to fly to the UK to pick up the Range Rover — the one that trumped da Vinci and Michelangelo in the interest stakes when we were at the Louvre. But he stays with me one last night, in a cute Airbnb in the seventeenth *arrondissement*. Our French village friends later frown at this choice, claiming the seventeenth is not safe, but I put this down to provincial nervousness about big cities, especially the idea of straying away from tourist spots. But hey, what do I know? I am perhaps not seeing things clearly either, because I am intoxicated. Drunk on the joy of being in a city. A real city. Sorry, Auckland... you mean well, but Paris has a few years on you. Let's discuss this again in a century or so.

In Paris I am infatuated with it all — I see charm in everything, and the more working-class, down-to-earth seventeenth *arrondissement* is no exception. Our tiny apartment is up a winding, narrow wooden staircase with an old-fashioned iron-gated lift clanking up the centre. We have rented just the large double bedroom, with the owner occupying the rest. When I open the bedroom curtains, I am only a few feet from the opposite balcony where a curly-haired young man leans out, smoking a cigarette. He waves. This is many people's idea of hell, this cheek-by-jowl living. I just think, *Oh how Parisian!*

An apartment or indeed any dwelling is an identikit image, its contents forming a crude portrait of its inhabitant. I haven't met the owner yet, but going off the clues these lodgings give, I'm looking for an older woman with an artsy-boho vibe. Batiks, abstract landscapes and framed exhibition posters cover the walls; woven Peruvian-style blankets are draped over chairs; a teetering pile of papers threatens immediate chaos on the coffee table. On the numerous shelves, novels and cookbooks have shuffled up to make room for plants and there are bookshelf escapees everywhere: here a hardback on Frida Kahlo; there a French copy of *Sapiens*; on the sofa, a Stephen King novel. This woman, I hazard, will be busy, curious and definitely make her own soup.

How wonderful, to live like this. Cocooned in your memories and experiences, reminders of who you are all around you. I feel guilty, like I am cheating in my thoughts on both Alistair and the *moulin*. But really . . . I can see myself here: free, independent, the underground *métro* laying the whole city at my feet.

But I can't become a Tumbleweed, blown from one adventure to another. I can't be seduced by another dream, not while this one is still unfinished business. For now at least, my path is with Alistair. And a *bistro* beckons.

———————

Early next morning, Alistair pops a quick kiss on my forehead, endearingly pulls the bed covers up to my chin so I stay warm; and sneaks out quietly. I luxuriate in my duvet nest for a while, then get up to shower, dress and head out in search of breakfast. The street is lively, Friday-morning commuters hurrying to a soundtrack of police sirens and car horns, and I duck into a large, empty *brasserie* on the corner by the underground station. Settling myself in a seat by the window, I drink my *café au lait*, butter my *croissant* and watch Paris pull up its blinds, lay out its stalls and prepare itself for another day.

Forty-five years, I muse, *since I sat alone in a Parisian café like this. But oh how fast life rushes past, how impatient it is to get somewhere.* It frightens me, this headlong, ever-quickening dash. So I order another coffee and sip it slowly, as if to rein in time.

11

'O Christmas Tree'

'What do you mean you don't like Christmas?' I say, bemused.

I've heard this claim before, of course. Many times. But I always thought it was posturing, a way of showing how much more depth you have. A kind of, 'Look, tinsel-brain, some of us see right through that bullshit.' I mean, I get it. It's tacky and consumerist. But heavens, what isn't? In London a few years ago, I even spotted a 'Meditation Shop'. If they can strew the path to enlightenment with 'must-have products', they can commercialise anything.

Plus, in the bigger scheme of things, amid all the truly hideous crimes of capitalism, do we really have time to hate on a few plastic baubles and a bit of fake snow?

Alistair, however, seems to be genuinely offended by the whole concept of Christmas. Not just the forced cheer, unnecessary expense and raft of God-awful romcoms (his opinion, not mine). He's also had too many miserable Christmasses, he explains, so he'd rather not celebrate it at all, thank you very much.

The problem with arguing *for* Christmas if you are not religious is that you end up sounding like a materialistic fool.

Yet in our family, Christmas has always been a big deal. Up until a few years ago (sorry girls), my daughters would sleep under the tree on Christmas Eve. They are in their twenties. The tradition of buying them new pyjamas to wear for the occasion has continued even though the girls waking up on Christmas morning covered in pine needles has not. We always have an advent calendar (a wooden one like a house that I place gifts in); we buy the biggest possible tree we can shoe-horn into my tiny Nissan (which has been known to sport reindeer antlers) and I'm a sucker for a bit of yuletide schmaltz of the *Love Actually* kind.

Growing up in the inclement English north, *of course* I'm a fan of the festive season. I associate Christmas with the one bright spot in long, bleak winters where even the snow was the colour of old undies. I nurse fond memories of the *Morecambe and Wise Christmas Show*; carol singers on the doorstep and sculpting fat men with carrot noses from fresh-fallen snow. I recall the satisfaction of getting our arthritic nutcrackers to actually deliver on their promise; the thrill of leafing through the Christmas *TV Times* (we weren't posh enough to get it all year round) and eating After Eights in front of a blazing fire. Hell, I even loved midnight Mass. Especially in my teens, when my friends and I would spend the night drinking in the Stanford Arms then head to our school chapel for the late service, offering up Bacardi-and-Coke breath to the new Lord Jesus. And ogling the talent from the local Catholic boys' school.

After moving to New Zealand, I bleated along with the rest of my fellow UK migrants that 'Christmas just isn't the same in summer'. I soon got over that. Rather than resenting our new environment for not being cold, dark and miserable enough, we made other traditions: those that embraced the climate. We strolled along Franklin Road every Christmas Eve, delighting in the late-evening warmth and ever more ambitious lighting displays festooning residents' homes and gardens. On Christmas Day itself, we swam at Takapuna Beach, no matter the weather, then ate our picnic under the pōhutukawa, reading our brand-new Christmas books. We had dinner late then played board games long into the evening. A family of happy, sated, slightly tipsy nerds.

So the idea of spending my first-ever Christmas away from my daughters in a wintry stone turret devoid of all celebration . . . well, it's unthinkable.

———————

Alistair is unwell. Really unwell. My initial diagnosis is Man Flu — but I ask my Nicer Self for a second opinion. Yep, it's the real thing. Not Man Flu but an equal-opportunity illness, available to both sexes. Fever, snuffles, coughs, the works. It probably doesn't help that we've just attended a Christmas market wearing inadequate clothing for the time of year. The snow swirled around us in little fluffy morsels, and we ooh-ed and ah-ed and froze our butts off. We came home with some locally made *Chabichou* (cheese made from goat's milk); a soft woollen mustard-coloured scarf; a green and orange woven shopping basket; and for Alistair, a dose of lurgy.

I feel for Alistair, I really do. And as the *moulin*'s chief nurse, I take my duties seriously. I make soup, grate fresh ginger into hot lemon drinks, and take care of the house while he stays under the duvet for a full week, building his own snowman of tissues next to the bed.

But Christmas is only a few days away and I don't want to spend it like Bob Cratchit, tending to a sickly child and thinking of all the festive revelry taking place elsewhere. Most of all, I'm honestly scared the homesickness will crank up several notches, that the gloom will take hold and never let go; so I launch my Christmas offensive: gently, of course. I sit on the edge of the bed, pat Alistair's hot hand, and inquire sweetly: 'Al, darling, I know it's not really your thing but how about a small tree?' He agrees, through coughs, that a bit of festive foliage will do no harm.

I've noticed several small pine trees appearing outside shops and cafés, unadorned, just sort of standing there like bushy green security guards. I suggest we nick one, because the store owners don't even bring them inside after hours. Alistair says that is very un-Christmassy of me (which is confusing from someone who personifies non-Christmas) and that these trees are there for public enjoyment. They're not really exuding any joy, is my point. Anyway, I don't pilfer one. I head to the garden centre and purchase the cutest, most perfectly cone-shaped little green beauty and several sets of lights. She may be small, but she's going to rock more bling than a Kardashian.

The tree ends up being our only Christmas decoration. But she punches above her weight. Even Alistair, now up and about but still a bit wobbly, is smitten. At night, when we switch off all the living-room lamps, she dazzles solo like the Eiffel Tower. And whenever I return to the mill in the dark, she guides me down the driveway towards our *moulin*-turned-lighthouse — just one small square of window flashing blue, red, yellow and green. Beckoning me home.

With Alistair in bed early of an evening, I binge on all my old favourite seasonal films — *The Holiday*, *Elf*, *The Apartment* and the Christmas episodes of *Friends* and even *The OC*. Then I make my bed up on the sofa, and fall asleep contentedly by the soft glow of the dying embers.

Alistair may not love Christmas, but he does love good baking. So we order a cake and mince pies from Carolyn — she of the curtains. Carolyn is English, speaks fluent French, has a full-time job as a carer for the elderly, runs a sewing business on the side, renovated her house with her own hands, and makes the best damn Christmas cake I have ever tasted. It's moist, boozy, just the right amount of fruit. The mince pies are to die for, too. I'm considering asking Carolyn to marry me but (a) she's taken,

(b) I'm taken, and (c) her brilliance at absolutely everything would start to get annoying.

Next, we turn our thoughts to the day itself. Christmas *à deux* could be cosy and romantic. Then again, it could be a washout. What with me and the homesickness and Alistair just plain sick. I toss up the probability of magic versus tragic and decide what's needed is some *bonhomie* of La Petite Auberge kind.

A welcoming space of red-checked tablecloths, low wood-beamed ceilings and tiled floors, this local family-run *bistro* is offering a five-course Christmas Day lunch for just 50 euros. The place exudes friendliness and warmth, with genial wait-staff and a chef–owner who makes a point of coming out to chat to customers. If you can't feel the yuletide spirit here, then God help you. Our friends Marianne and Tony have already booked and want us to join them, assuring us it's *the* place to be on Christmas Day. It's probably also *the* only place open, but whatever. We're in.

Christmas morning turns out to be far cheerier than I had anticipated. Alistair and I exchange gifts and he is thrilled with the Peugeot pepper mill I bought for him in Paris. It's a thing of sleek beauty, a stainless steel and glass cylinder that lights up when you press the top to grind the peppercorns. He'd waxed lyrical to me about these pepper grinders a while back; only an engineer could be so in raptures over the design of a condiment dispenser. Alistair buys me much-needed earbuds, and two pairs of denim dungarees. Now I am truly kitted out for the rural 'good life'.

My daughters video-call so we can open each other's gifts 'live on air'. Lucy has bought me a gorgeously soft jumper the colour of crushed raspberries. Su has gifted me a button-up black velvet dress with a belt that fits perfectly. While I am still half-stupid from sleep, they are lively and refreshed after their day at the beach. In the background the dog is chewing wrapping paper, the cat is hissing at the dog, the girls' dad is bustling around muttering and clattering pans, and it's the usual 25 December chaos. Something about the scene reassures me. That sense of continuity. This is the way it always was. It's not like the minute I left New Zealand everything I cherished simply evaporated into thin air. It will all still be there when I go back.

———————

It's touch and go as to whether we will make it to lunch, with Alistair still feeling iffy and devoid of appetite. It's ironic that now he is finally embracing Christmas, Alistair looks about as ho-ho-ho as a stale mince pie. Pale, still coughing (it's not Covid) and moving sluggishly, he nonetheless insists that we keep our date with the *auberge*. Which is just as well because all we have at home is that Christmas cake, a few mince pies and a cupboard full of booze.

We arrive at twelve to find a restaurant packed with families and kids of all ages. Sharing our table — alongside Marianne and Tony — are a quiet English couple who have kindly brought

Christmas crackers, not something the French are familiar with. Also joining us are their 23-year-old son and his girlfriend. The young couple cheerfully announce that they are supremely hungover and close to collapse, having got home at 4 a.m. You wouldn't know it. She especially looks radiant, and he tucks into all five courses with gusto.

Ah yes, about those five courses. Okay, well slip into something loose because even reading this menu may make your waistband feel uncomfortable.

First, a *mise en bouche* — literally a 'pop-in-the-mouth'. It's not even a starter, but a warm-up for the starter. Here it's a *Velouté de Châtaigne aux St Jacques* — a small chestnut dish with a velvety purée texture. Next an *entrée* double act: *Tourte de Canard au Foie-gras avec Terrine de Homard et Langoustines aux Agrumes*. I give the duck-in-pastry with *foie gras* and lobster terrine a miss. Both to conserve my appetite and, while I have become a meat-eater again in France, I draw the line at force-feeding geese and torturing crustaceans. The second *entrée* I dive into — a *Cocotte de la Mer avec Bar, Gambas, Moules, Coques and Lotte*. This sublime casserole contains bass, prawns, mussels, cockles and monkfish. Alistair picks at his, driven less by appetite and more by a fear of missing out.

The main course is a mouthful even to say — *Filet de Bœuf aux Fruits Secs et Jus de Truffes et Brochettes de Filets de Caille, Sauce Miel et Tomates Confites, Endives Braisées, Écrasé de Pommes de Terre aux Cèpes et Mirepoix de Légumes*. In short, a party-in-the-mouth of meltingly soft beef fillet, tender quail, a honey-based tomatoey sauce, braised endives, a creamy potato purée and sautéed mixed vegetables with herbs. A *mirepoix*, incidentally, involves slowly cooking carrot, onion and celery in oil or butter to deepen and enrich their flavour. Never was a vegetable more luscious; not a sad grey sprout in sight. Hallelujah, hosanna and joy to the world.

But wait. Sit back down. There is more.

The cheese course. And *Plateau de Fromages* is an understatement if ever there was one. It's not a tray or board at all but an entire trolley-load — a creamy, pungent *fromage*-fest on wheels. All the usual suspects are there, plus a luscious white circle of *brie* the size of a dartboard. We each go up to the trolley and make our selection. I want a *tranche* of that *brie*, but when the wait-person cuts into it she gives a little start, accompanied by an 'Ew'. I lean forward to peer at the cheese, in trepidation, but the source of her alarm is nothing more than a dark seam of truffle running through the creamy centre. Perhaps this young woman needs to re-think her job options. If you like your cheeses tame and predictable, like a smooth slab of Edam, then you're in no position to be manning a French *fromage* trolley.

Et finalement — a trio of desserts. *Chou Craquelin Mousse Chocolat; Vacherin aux Fruits Rouges; Poire Pochée aux Épices.* It's a tribute to the chef that we polish off our plates, Alistair excluded. I can just about fit in an espresso at the end, then waddle to the car — woozy on wine and stuffed to the earrings. In my new velvet dress, I arrived at the restaurant black and slender as an exclamation mark and now feel rotund as a closing bracket. And this is the upside to a cold-weather Christmas; with no beach parading to be done, all of this extra food is just between me and my loosened belt. Nothing to see here.

––––––––

In the days following Christmas, Alistair and I are hopping with excitement about our upcoming trip. The trouble is, we are not hopping with excitement about the *same* upcoming trip.

Unable to resist the urge any longer, I have booked a flight to New Zealand for February. Just a visit, mind. Alistair has kindly loaned me the money because I am all yearning and no liquid assets. It's all I can think about. Actually hugging my beautiful children, squeezing their cheeks (yes I still do that), scratching the dog behind his ears, returning to my favourite beaches — both exhilarated and apprehensive about dipping beneath the chilly waves for the first time. Tides of discomfort and joy; there's almost a carol in there.

Alistair meanwhile is feverishly leafing through road guides to Spain, planning an itinerary for our New Year roadie. We will be heading down through south-eastern France — stopping in Carcassonne, then Collioure just shy of the Spanish border — and on down the east coast of Spain. I'm looking forward to this trip too, but not quite as effervescently as Alistair would like. In hindsight, I can see his disappointment. This is THE point of living in France: access to the wonders of Europe. Back in Auckland I had talked with misty eyes of my connection to

Spain. My South American mum lived in Andalucia, in the south, for 30 years after my dad died, and I spent many a happy summer with her. In my twenties, I spent an entire year teaching English in Málaga.

Alistair is planning and booking and poring over maps, and I should be cheerleading his efforts more. But I can't.

It's not that I am ungrateful. But my enthusiasm is considerably corseted by the fact I have no money to contribute to this odyssey. I am earning very little by this point. My regular freelance work from New Zealand has slowed to a trickle, and it's hard to summon up any zeal about a trip where you feel like a financial leper. Because that's how I feel. Alistair is kindly paying for the accommodation, and it sucks. It's not like being a student, travelling on a shoestring with your mates. There, you are all in the same boat. Or rather the same flea-infested hostel. It's a laugh, it's your last go at slumming it before you become a proper Grown Up. But now I *am* a proper Grown Up. A vintage one at that. One of the things I love about Alistair is his enthusiasm, and right now I wish I could offer up an equally hearty 'Let's go halves!' or even 'Why don't we stay here — my treat!' But I can't, and my powerlessness translates into passivity. Which Alistair takes as ungratefulness.

When the day itself arrives and the Range Rover is stuffed like a post-Christmas turkey with bags, hats, shoes, books, baskets and suitcases, I am still not doing cartwheels around the lawn. But now the lukewarm response is for another reason: I can hardly believe this is happening. That we are leaving the cold and the grey and in just a week, will be in Nerja, on Spain's beautiful southern coast.

As we head out of the *moulin* gates, it seems crazy that our rock-strewn, muddy stretch of driveway is what connects us — albeit with thousands of miles in between — to Barcelona, Valencia, Málaga, Granada, Córdoba, the Basque Country.

I take a last look at the river. 'Bye bye Vienne — see you in three weeks.'

———————

In an attempt to detox from the excesses of Christmas, a few days before our trip Alistair and I have started fasting. Not drastically so, just leaving a wider window between eating times. I mention this because after a couple of hours on the road, we spy an *aire* — one of the French autoroute service stations. *Aire* is a deceptive word. It suggests a patch of grass with picnic tables, a place of wholesomeness and simplicity. Some are indeed just that — the *aires de repos* are snippets of nature, often with toilets, where you can pull over so the kids can pee and fight in the fresh air rather than the car. But *aires de service* are full-on service stations with restaurants, gas pumps, toilets and shops full of merch.

The one we enter is of the latter sort. 'Are we still fasting?' I ask Alistair, wondering what the road-trip rules are. Fasting is a team sport — no sneaking off and wolfing a handful of peanuts while your partner is lying, listless as a wilted endive, on the sofa.

You have to have each other's backs. Now, however, Alistair answers not by replying, but by heading sleepwalker-like to the hot-food counter. It's as if he's being lured by cartoon-style tendrils of aroma, leading him by the nose to the fragrant casseroles and glossy sausages. It's just after 11 a.m., and now Alistair has on the tray in front of him a plate of thick, tomatoey beef *bourguignon*. No wine, although there is plenty on offer, and others are tucking in.

The sight makes me happy. This is holiday spirit at its finest.

Back in the car, after a good strong coffee and a *pain au chocolat*, I lean back and let the excitement belatedly take hold. The sun is out, we're heading south to Carcassonne, and even Alistair's on-rotation playing of Van Morrison cannot burst my bubble. We're on a road trip, baby!!

12

Are We There Yet?

After a journey that takes us through pottery (Limoges) and fine fabric (Tulle), we arrive at the hilltop fortress city of Carcassonne. Way down in France's south-east, Carcassonne is a bit of a show-stopper. It's a UNESCO World Heritage Site, and from first glimpse, you can see why. The three kilometres of thick walls and multiple watch towers have 'Don't Mess with Me' written all over them. They're awe-inspiring, for sure, but I don't warm to this initial impression of Carcassonne. Essentially a big scowl made of stone, the walls give me a *frisson*. And not the good kind.

Buildings do carry an energy, I believe, holding the past in their stones. And with a history as bloody as that of Carcassonne it is no wonder the fortress exudes bad vibes.

Dating all the way back to pre-Roman times, it's one of the best-preserved fortified medieval citadels on the planet and has been the site of many stormings, sieges and battles. Visigoths, Franks and Saracens were just some of the many testosterone-crazed hordes who at various times took the city, surrendered it, held it under siege, slaughtered and were slaughtered. In the thirteenth century, Carcassonne and much of the Languedoc (southern France) were seen as nests of heresy, as they were home to a Christian sect called the Cathars, who believed the material world was evil. It didn't pay to be different back then, especially when your differences put you at odds with the Catholic Church. The Vatican was mightily pissed off with the Cathars and their po-faced brand of worship. Because no one likes preachy do-gooders telling you your golden candlesticks, marble altars, and silk and ermine robes are the work of the devil. Can you imagine someone coming into your house, taking one look at your De'Longhi coffee maker and calmly informing you that you will burn in hell? Exactly. So yes, a big army was dispatched on the Pope's orders and 20,000 Cathars were killed in Béziers (80 kilometres from Carcassonne) during the Albigensian Crusade. Killed, mind — not murdered. And crusade, not genocide. I'm just doing some belated PR for the Vatican. After all, he was called Pope Innocent III, so it can't possibly have been his fault.

Next the army turned its attention to Carcassonne. The soldiers held the town under siege rather than destroy it as they quite sensibly reasoned it would be no good to them as rubble. So yes, the fact we can admire this magnificent fortress today is all thanks to some big hairy medieval dudes with zero compassion but a truckload of foresight.

My not warming to Carcassonne may also be down to the fact Alistair and I get off on a bad footing. A silly, silly thing — miscommunication as always. Plus Alistair is tired and I am hungry. We grown-ups really do underestimate the role physical discomfort plays in arguments. As adults, we believe we are so sophisticated; just because we subscribe to *The New Yorker*, can read a wine list and own a leaf-blower, we seem to believe we are exceptionally evolved. We are essentially toddlers. We don't recognise the triggers that will send us (figuratively) lying on the floor refusing to breathe until it's too late. So Alistair is exhausted but hasn't said so, and I am not at my best. It's not just hunger actually — something else is bothering me, but for the moment it's lurking in my peripheral vision. There is a lot of pressure on us to have a good time on this trip, to bond more deeply, to get our romantic shit together. Here we are, doing the thing we both came to Europe to do, so if we can't get along in this context, then God help us.

After dropping our bags at the hotel, we go down to the lobby and grab some tourist maps of the old town. Out on the street, Alistair says some words I don't quite catch and strides away round the back of the hotel, in the direction of where we've parked the car. Assuming he's gone to retrieve something, I wait for him by the hotel door. It is a long wait. By the time we meet up again, a good 25 minutes later, we are both exasperated. Alistair: 'I thought you were following me!' Me:'I am not a bloody chihuahua!' which is my admittedly bizarre way of saying I take exception to the assumption that I will just obediently trot after him, especially when he marches off with no explanation.

It is a small incident, but an important one. Because what happens next says a lot about our dynamic. A dynamic that is becoming a pattern. Rather than laughing about what a Laurel and Hardy show we are, and moving on, we sling our resentments over our shoulders and haul them along with us. Into my package of resentment I also throw a couple of extras: Alistair, you drive too fast. Alistair, I cannot listen to one more second of Van Morrison.

We begin to explore the town slightly separately from one another, always a few paces away. It's sad and it's lonely. One of us should approach the other, and quietly slip a hand in a hand. Plant a gentle kiss. But neither of us does.

I blame Carcassonne. Something hangs heavy in the air, and it's like having a big sulky child with us.

Back at the hotel, we talk about it. Alistair doesn't like that I 'start to rage' at the drop of a hat. I don't like that I am expected to second-guess his intentions, and that I can't even express annoyance without being accused of being a rabid, frothing-at-the-mouth, certifiable loony. Outwardly, I am angry. Actually I am terrified. My heart is racing, the old fears are hammering at the door. *What if this is it, what if this is the beginning of the end?* When I start to cry, Alistair comes over and puts his arms around me. My heart slows, my breath calms. His warm, ursine hug shuts out all the fear. And even though it's never wise to make someone else your fortress, for now I feel safe.

The Collioure of Memory

Next stop, Collioure. Ah Collioure. Last time I was here was 26 years ago: with my ex-husband, not long after we first met. I fell in love with the beautiful little Mediterranean port town, and a second visit doesn't change my mind. Collioure is just 25 kilometres north of the Spanish border, and the influence of her southern neighbour is all around us. It's in the snatches of Spanish conversation overheard in shops and at café tables, it's in the liveliness of the streets, in the packed restaurants — their clientele spilling onto outdoor terraces, where brisk waiters ferry enormous dishes of grilled *boquerones* (anchovies) and plates of golden, seafood-rich *paella*.

We sit at a table by the glinting harbour, me sipping on a *Banyuls* — a sweet, fortified wine-style *apéritif* — and Alistair a cold beer. The green coat is draped over the back of my chair, just to show this glorious winter weather that I am not taking it for granted. The sun is on our faces and we are in heaven. We finish our drinks, snap a few silly selfies — and there's not a Carcassonne-style cloud in sight.

The road to our next destination, the Catalonian town of Sitges on Spain's eastern coast, is one long line of beauty: the distant outline of the Pyrénées wearing a faint dusting of snow; miles and miles of vineyards; here and there terracotta-roofed villages clinging to the hillsides; slender paintbrush-shaped cypresses; and so many *châteaux* we stop oohing and aahing each and every time, a silent 'ditto' hanging in the air.

The border town of Le Perthus is an assault on the eyes in comparison, with its loud shop-front signs advertising duty-free liquor and bargain clothing. But after the next set of toll booths, I squeal with delight. On a sign in front of us, on an enormous blue background in a circle of stars, is a word that makes my heart do a quick *paso doble*. ESPAÑA.

––––––––––

A Train Ride and a Time Machine

After a three-day drive that traces Spain's eastern coastline, stopping off in Sitges and Alicante, we arrive in Nerja on the Costa del Sol. We are to stay here for two weeks, in a hilltop apartment with a balcony the size of a living room. Every morning we look out from our eyrie to the electric-blue ocean, down onto the whitewashed walls of the town and the bougainvillea-clad villas with their pools — rectangles of turquoise stamped on the landscape like 'well done!' stickers.

The highlight of this stay is not Nerja itself but a trip to Los Boliches, an hour's bus and train ride to the west. This is where I lived for a year with my mother when I was 22. My father had just died, and my Latin American mum found solace being in a Spanish-speaking environment that was near enough to her adopted home in the UK. Riding along the coast now with Alistair, I'm not on a train at all; I'm in a time machine.

We meet up with my friends from 40 years ago, at a *chiringuito* (a bar–restaurant right on the beach). After a long, long lunch with lots of reminiscing, laughing and catching up, we hug goodbye and Alistair and I head to the main plaza. This is the real reason for this pilgrimage. In the square is the church that was my mother's second home, and also a small silver plaque dedicated to her. It sits in a flowerbed on the high street edge of the square, and was the fruit of long pleading emails that my brother and I sent to the office of the mayor. Hers is the only plaque here; they made an exception. We desperately wanted her to leave a footprint in a place that meant so much to her, and where she gave so much back. She was in the choir, taught catechism, and put in many hours helping struggling new immigrants to the area — many of them from her homeland.

'Light a candle for Glorita,' my sister-in-law had said. 'When you're in there, light a candle.' I flinched momentarily at the suggestion, not being religious. But my sister-in-law is, and she loved my mum to bits, so it seems churlish not to comply. I install Alistair in a bar on the square with a small glass of brandy and head off in the direction of the church.

Grieving is a funny thing. It's more than ten years since my mum died and I miss her in that slightly distanced, academic way that you do, with time. But approaching the great wooden church doors as dusk falls, I feel like I have lost her all over again. In this place where she shone, this small peacock of a woman in high heels who knew everyone, her absence is tangible.

Inside, a small service is taking place, a woman in the pulpit quietly reading to the scant audience. Through an archway at the back of the church, I see candles flickering. Bracing myself for an emotionally and spiritually charged moment, I walk quietly towards them and prepare to light my taper. But no. The candles are under glass, and they are electric. There is a slot to put your money in. I pop in two euros and give a little start as some twelve candles burst into life at once. It's like the dance floor from *Saturday Night Fever*. And this makes me so happy. For a lady who lit up the room, disco candles are just perfect.

———————

I have to leave Nerja for three days to fly to London. It's not ideal, but the mother of one of my closest friends has died, and Tricia is in pieces. Her mum and dad were beautiful individuals who provided a home away from home for me and my brother after my mother moved to Spain. It's only right that I should be there to support a dear friend, and say goodbye to someone who showed me so much kindness.

Alistair cannot fathom it. He has planned this lovely trip and here I am abandoning him for three days. 'Tell her you're on holiday!' he insists. 'She will understand.' I haven't told Tricia I am on a road trip and don't intend to, because this is not about me. But on this subject Alistair and I aren't just on a different page, we aren't even reading the same book. As I see it, it's a duty to someone I care deeply about. Alistair, perhaps not realising just how important Tricia is to me, regards it as supremely selfish — as being uncaring towards him.

I arrive back at Málaga airport on Sunday night and take the bus to Nerja. Alistair picks me up in town and drives us back to the apartment. I am hurt that he didn't offer to meet me off the plane. It would have been a lengthy drive, but that doesn't usually faze Alistair. I feel he is making a point, punishing me in some way. Perhaps I am being childish. I honestly don't know anymore.

———

In the movies, road trips are always revelatory. Even if they involve armed hold-ups, or family tragedy, as in the fabulous *Little Miss Sunshine*, the protagonists are invariably moving towards something other than their destination. They are making important discoveries about themselves, about each other.

Our road trip is nothing like this. We'll have a great day, then an argument, followed by tension, then another great day, more falling out, more tension. There's a sense of us clocking up plenty of miles but making little ground as a couple. Plus, while I'm immensely grateful to Alistair for spending long hours at the wheel, more often than not he scares the bejesus out of me. He goes at quite a clip, and the Range Rover's body language towards slower drivers is often, shall we say, a *soupçon* overbearing. I'm happiest when I am sleeping, or writing on my laptop in the back, oblivious to motorway perils.

On our best days there's a lightness between us, an easy play-fulness. At these times, our private world and the public-facing one are aligned. The Instagram posts of us hugging and laughing aren't a front; they're an accurate representation of two people in harmony. But then there are the awful moments I never see coming, the fiery arguments and freezing silences. It's like standing in a clear blue ocean, gazing in joy and wonder at the tiny darting fish . . . then WHAM, a huge wave knocks you over, and you feel foolish for ever having let your guard down.

Strangely, after those episodes, when we've glimpsed how truly desolate we can make each other feel, we cling more des-perately to the relationship. To the narrative that we set out to create. We must keep going.

———————

Ávila. Another walled fortress city, just north-west of Madrid, and it couldn't be more different to Carcassonne. There is nothing sinister or oppressive here — apart from the snow-threatening sky. Ávila's 2.5 kilometres of medieval walls flow like a silver ribbon around the old city, stoic and graceful.

For our second night in Ávila, I do a wild, reckless thing. Well, reckless for someone on a fourteen-hours-a-week wage. But who can say no to the chance to stay in a sixteenth-century palace? Not me, it turns out. I treat Alistair and I to a night at the *parador* inside the old city and in fact it's only moderately reckless (if there can be such a thing). *Paradores* are the best thing since sliced *chorizo*. These state-run hotels are magnificent properties — castles, mansions, monasteries, fortresses, convents, historic buildings, aforementioned palaces — which combine the best of historic atmosphere with modern comfort. And they're subsidised by the government, which means the more monetarily challenged among us can enjoy a bit of luxe at a relatively modest price.

This *parador*, formerly the Palace of Piedras Albas, isn't just within Ávila's historic walls. It is part of them, built into the second line of the city's defences. So from the outside, we're well fortified. Not that we're expecting a coachload of Visigoths anytime soon. But best to be prepared. On the inside, we're fortified too . . . by a well-stocked bar and hands-down THE best hot chocolate that has ever passed my lips and broken down my healthy-eating defences. I reckon had they poured this stuff over invaders rather than shooting arrows at them, their foes would have been too busy licking it off each other to think about fighting. Then they would have waddled away like fat happy cats to sleep it off in the sun. Spanish hot chocolate is thick, rich, molten velvet. It's usually made with dark chocolate, cornflour, sugar and maybe a dash of milk. Clean eating it is not. But there is a level of divinity in food and drink where 'Oh I shouldn't' doesn't even come into it. It would be like someone saying to you 'Would you care to look at the *Mona Lisa*?' and your reply is 'I couldn't possibly — I already had three Caravaggios.' This hot chocolate is a thing of beauty, of culinary perfection so elevated that to NOT indulge would be perverse. So we polish off this heaven-in-a-cup with light, fluffy madeleines and not a word of regret or remorse is spoken between us.

So this is our journey. A *chiaroscuro* painting, thick with drama and emotion but shot through with the occasional burst of light. If one word were to sum up my state of mind at the end of the holiday, it would surely be 'perplexed'. The episodes of alienation on both our parts . . . they make no sense alongside those moments of joy, the very fact that Alistair and I can be so utterly transfixed by one another.

In Donostia-San Sebastián, near the end of an evening of superb *tapas* and wine in the Basque city's old quarter, Alistair decides to do a 'video interview' with me about the evening. I start waxing lyrical about *tapas* but have to keep asking him to stop because I am laughing too much to carry on.

Watching his expression, the 'Oh my God you're a nutter but I love you' look on his face, I feel a tug of longing. Wanting to keep this Alistair, this moment, forever.

And yet a far greater tug of longing will take me away from him just two weeks later.

13

Another Road Trip

As the date of my departure for Auckland draws near, I start to worry. And all because of a French government pension reform.

A few weeks ago, I made a remark to Alistair about an article I was reading in *Libération*, France's left-wing national newspaper (co-founded by philosopher Jean-Paul Sartre, no less, in the early 1970s as a true democratic publication, for and by the people). If that sounds pretentious, you'd be right. Because while 'reading a French newspaper' makes it seem like I am terribly erudite, the truth is I had subscribed to *Libération* months earlier but had scarcely glanced at it. The intention was to stay abreast of current affairs *and* improve my French at the same time. Except to date I'd read precisely one book review, and one celebrity interview with an actor from a French Netflix drama.

But on this occasion, I *was* actually engrossed in something serious. It was an article about growing nationwide unrest over what the French see as a slap in the face to workers' rights. President Emmanuel Macron — using executive powers to push the law through, further fanning the flames of indignation — was planning to raise the retirement age from 62 to 64. That's right, the French retire at 62. The general response, when I tell this to people in New Zealand and the UK, is 'What the hell are they complaining about? Even sixty-four is lower than most countries!' But I see the protesters' point. The retirement age was 60, until President Nicolas Sarkozy nudged it up to 62, back in 2010. You can see what's happening here. It's not just about numbers, but *direction*. No one wants to see their rights going backwards. I'm with them.

What in God's name did all this have to do with me going to Auckland? Strikes. Train strikes, to be more exact. The French are consummate protesters, and when they are *emmerdés* (pissed off) they don't just sign petitions, change their Facebook profile picture frame, or write letters in capitals to their MP (all perfectly fine, by the way). They get properly angry. They take action, as they should. So yes, a few weeks ago I was saying 'Go the workers!' to Alistair. Right now, trying to get to Paris airport only to find the trains are not running, I'd like to amend my proletarian cheerleading to 'Go the workers! But not on Tuesday, please.'

My flight leaves Charles de Gaulle for Auckland at 6 p.m., and trains are looking very patchy. So I have booked a bus to get me to Paris the evening before, staying overnight at a hotel near the airport. I am not looking forward to the journey, especially the bit where I have to figure out how to get from the bus drop-off point in the city to the airport hotel, quite a distance away. The details of this are still murky, and may involve an expensive cab ride and / or a futile search for buses.

Alistair has said very little. He's usually the human equivalent of a Swiss army knife, with solutions for practically everything. He is also incredibly proactive, so would normally be busily helping me to investigate the best routes. I'm not about to ask him for help, determined to figure it out myself — as a reminder that I was a fully functioning member of society before I met him and quite capable of cracking this problem. But also, given that Alistair is so unhappy about my departure, it doesn't seem fair to make him an accomplice in it.

I am fossicking around in bags and doing last-minute double and triple checks. Then Alistair says something entirely unexpected. 'I will drive you. To Paris.'

I don't even bother with the usual niceties of 'Ooh, are you sure; no, I couldn't possibly . . .' From me, it's an instant 'Oh that would be incredible!'

Going in the car with Alistair is not just logistically life-saving. It means he and I get to have a little more time together. He will stay with me at the hotel and leave for home again the next morning.

Visually, this journey couldn't be more different to our three-week jaunt. No beautiful coastline, no stunning mountain ranges, no idyllic restaurants, no azure skies — just bad-tempered grey clouds, traffic jams, and urban sprawl for miles and miles as we approach Paris. It's by no means an Instagrammable 'dream trip'. Yet here's the funny thing. It's magical. It's everything our big roadie should have been. We chat more, we laugh more. Alistair is still driving fast, but for some reason it's not making me wish I had made a will, nor am I clutching at the roof handles. The fact we're not navigating bendy Spanish coastal roads but a simple stretch of motorway may come into it. But also I'm just generally more relaxed.

We stop off at a service station and act like a couple of clowns, trying on ridiculous sunnies and picking out hypothetical presents for one another. I threaten to buy Alistair a giant, grotesque Eiffel Tower ornament; he insists on reciprocating with a truly hideous paperweight.

Everything about the trip feels light, playful, absurd. We're like two runaway kids relishing their shared adventure, rather than lovers with a turbulent dynamic about to be separated for quite some time. Perhaps we can be like this because the pressure is off. This is essentially a long commute, not a 'bucket list' tour of Spain. So this, apparently, is what we need to thrive . . . a terrain devoid of expectation.

Our hotel is a huge slab of a building, a U-shaped multi-storeyed edifice wrapped around a broad courtyard. It's a few kilometres from the airport itself, but it feels like we're sleeping at the end of the runway; just outside our window the control tower blinks at us like a giant alarm clock. The hotel seems perfectly fine — in a clean, modern, faceless sort of way. But there's a shiftiness about it that I can't quite put my finger on. The staff appear to be pretending, like this isn't really a hotel at all. When Alistair asks how he will get out of the car park in the morning (the gate is locked), they seem genuinely surprised at the question, as if no one has ever wanted to leave before. They should change the name to Hotel California.

For our last night together, we head to a little Italian restaurant — improbably down a couple of desolate, dimly lit streets near the hotel. It feels like the restaurant at the end of the universe, the only other buildings being some modest bungalows and that control tower. Over pasta carbonara and a *pichet* of *rosé,* we have the strangest conversation. If you wrote it as dialogue for a movie, people would say, 'Well that was weird; no one talks like that.' It's Alistair who sets the tone, telling me how much he loves 98 per cent of me. But there's a 2 per cent (is there some kind of online calculator for this I don't know about?) that is impossible. That 2 per cent Maria is too angry, and (he does at least have the decency to pause here) . . . actually quite mad. I'm not sure where he is going with this, whether he is about to break up with me or whether I should focus on the 98 per cent, but the strange part is I am not upset or offended. Nor is there any acrimony in Alistair's words. They are spoken gently, without vehemence. He actually sounds rather disappointed in himself. Perhaps his engineer's brain has kicked in, and he is merely frustrated because the answer to the problem in front of him — i.e., me — is *almost* within his grasp. Except for that 2 per cent.

I express a few things I'm not thrilled about either. How he sometimes seems so distant, unreachable. He nods and listens. It's the first time we've spoken this openly without one of us triggering the other. We just speculate and explore, poking and picking over the relationship gently, with curiosity, as if we were sharing a plate of salad and trying to get to the olives. It's reminiscent of a scene in a Murakami novel — both hyperreal (the uncomfortable chairs; the noisy crowd in the corner; the thick pasta sauce) and dreamlike (the location; my imminent departure; this new dynamic between us). If someone had wandered over and said, 'Coffee is being served at the end of the runway,' I wouldn't have been surprised. Life gives us these moments — surreal morsels plucked straight out of dreams, with no rhyme or reason, just an overwhelming sensation that has no name. A sensation containing too many ingredients to fit on one label. Sadness, bewilderment, tenderness . . . a sudden desire to laugh.

The next morning, the surreality continues. Entering the 'dining room' in search of breakfast, we find it is dark and empty. Against one wall is a forlorn-looking coffee machine, the sort you get in hospitals. Oh, and a giant stuffed squirrel. Honestly, no idea.

So sitting on a sofa in reception with a terrible cup of coffee and just a few feet from an enormous stuffed rodent, we say goodbye. Alistair is talking about his route home, and looking at traffic reports, but I am only half-listening. I am nestled into his lapel, letting the tears soak into the thick fabric.

And then the airport shuttles arrives.

14

Kia Ora, Auckland

'I've got to decide one way or another. I can't keep trading hemispheres and sadnesses,' I tell my friend Mary.

'Ooh, that's *good*,' she says. 'Trading hemispheres and sadnesses. Write it down.' She's not looking at me, but sorting through a huge cardboard box of old letters, theatre programmes, cinema tickets, newspaper clippings and other life paraphernalia: special moments immortalised as creased, faded bits of paper.

Mary is trying to do a long-overdue clear-out (her words) so she can put her house on the market. But she is an even worse procrastinator than I am. Safe to say, if there was a category in the New Zealander of the Year Awards for stalling, Mary would be a shoo-in. I love that about her though. She's not a rusher. She listens to what you've said, swills it around in her mind for a moment, and delivers a considered response. I know she isn't ignoring me right now, just temporarily distracted — and that's understandable. Deep-diving through your memories, that's a difficult thing to surface from.

And I am being no use to her at all. Having offered to help Mary sort her shit out (because frankly at this pace her home will not be ready for sale until 2050 — when most people will be living in floating e-pods high above the city), I am doing a jigsaw of Venice. It's truly beautiful; the deep turquoise of the canal, the last rays of sun saturating the *palazzo* walls, the glowing street lights . . . Procrastination is infectious, and the most common killer of productive time. There should be something you can take for it, if only because someone would have great fun coming up with a product name. Pro-Crash. Pro-Zap. Or something a bit more shouty, like those insect and household sprays you get — No More Delays!

It's already April, and I've been in Auckland since February. This was meant to be a holiday, but it has morphed into something else. I appear to be stuck in limbo. It takes little effort to reside in limbo; you don't need a visa, and you can stay as long as you like. I'd go so far as to say that it's a comfortable place to settle in — a neutral territory, like Switzerland, but cheaper. Alistair, understandably enough, is concerned. Every phone conversation starts with, 'So are you coming back?' 'Oh yes of course!' I always reply. I have left the green coat, precious family photos and a whole host of other items in France as a token of my intention to return. Hostages, you might say.

Mary looks up from her memory-wrangling. She has two boxes, one full of stuff still to be sorted through and another one for the 'rubbish'. The rubbish box has two bits of paper in it. Then there is a rather large mass on the floor in front of her, in neither box, and it looks suspiciously like an 'undecided' pile. Limbo is everywhere.

'So *are* you going back?' Mary asks, this time looking directly at me. Silence. I am turning my attention to the puzzle. And then: 'Yes!! . . . I finally found the gondolier's foot!!'

———————

It's not fair to Alistair to be so vague about my return date. And I do miss him. Despite the constant arguing, which in our last few weeks together — aside from that last road trip — showed no sign of abating. But I put a lot of this down to fear. Alistair has already lost one woman he loved, to cancer. He could see that I was pining for New Zealand, and the threat was always present that I would leave him too.

For my part, I have two contradictory fears. One, that the relationship will not work out, simply because they never have. Two, that the relationship will work out, which will mean spending a good part of my remaining years away from my daughters.

You may justifiably wonder why I left them in the first place. The answer is simple. I didn't realise it would be so hard. I swallowed everybody else's logic: 'Hey, they will be fine!! They are independent now, and look what a great example you are giving them! You know, really getting out of your comfort zone, showing that life can be lived at any age! And you can Zoom, right?' But of course it's not really the same. Zoom is a pathetic substitute for physical presence. When I arrived in Auckland for 'the holiday', I couldn't stop giving them sidelong looks in the car home from the airport, unable to believe they were really there. If you'd asked what the primary emotion was, when I saw them again, of course it was love. But at the time it felt more like relief. Now that we were all together, safely reunited, I could breathe.

———————

I end up staying in New Zealand for four months. Four happy months where I feel calm and at peace. Four months of dog walks, beach swims, family dinners and brunches, and catching up with close friends. It's great to be back in the office, too, rather than working remotely. I feel part of something. And there's more cake.

I keep reminding myself this is just a holiday, but it doesn't help that a dog-walking friend asks if I can house-sit for six weeks while she and her family take off to Europe. Of course I say yes. Her home is gorgeous: spacious, bright and modern with a pool, an adorable terrier and a cat that's Pixar-animation perfect. Yes, I could definitely live in Auckland, I think to myself . . . then the family returns, the spell is broken, and I remember that everything I own is in two suitcases.

———————

Auckland is a hard city to live in: the public transport is capricious, you can't buy a house, rents are astronomical, there is too much congestion and motorists *never* let you into the traffic. But I love it, nonetheless, and I greedily inhale every moment, every experience that I can't get in a riverside hamlet. My daughters buy us all tickets to a Harry Styles concert, as my birthday treat, and we dance so hard we can barely walk back to the car. I attend a rally for trans rights, which is more party than protest, and revel in the electric atmosphere and burst of colour. I join a gym, and start to notice some muscle tone returning to my arms — arms whose idea of a workout in France was carrying *baguettes* to the car. I enjoy long shoreline walks with the whippet, delight in being able to call up friends for wine, coffee or the movies. And I meet two brand-new humans: friends' babies who came into the world while I was on the other side of it.

———————

So why do I decide to go back to France?

Because I don't feel I have given the relationship a fair chance. Alistair has often accused me of still having one foot in New Zealand, and of course he is right. For all the reasons stated above, I haven't been able to let go. But a relationship is hard to let go of too. At 64, and after so many romantic failures, I don't want to simply toss this one in the too-hard basket. The thought torments me that perhaps I have never done the work necessary to make a relationship stick. I'd always believed 'It should be easy,' and if it wasn't easy, well, that showed it wasn't meant to be. But is that even true? Isn't that perhaps just an excuse, a way of avoiding the messy, painfully vulnerable business of truly getting close to someone? I don't want to be a quitter, I really don't.

I even pen a 'manifesto' for Alistair, outlining the things I could do to make our relationship better. He loves it, though he doesn't respond in kind. Here is an extract:

Being more couple-y (i.e. how to counter Maria's over-defensiveness)

I've realised I'm not actually good at being 'in a team' — in a relationship sense. And it's odd because I don't get all weird and independent around my friends. I think somewhere is a deep-seated fear that every romantic relationship is going to end anyway, so why make it more painful by surrendering my sense of self and then having to build it all back up again later on? This is crazy thinking, and actually ends up producing the very thing I feared in the first place. But emotions are not rational.

I need to realise that 'doing stuff together' isn't a threat to my very essence, but merely a lovely way to spend time with — and be present for — the person I have chosen to live my life with. As we discussed earlier, it's not about me making more time necessarily for you (though that would be nice), but being more open and intimate and emotionally available when we are together.

I need to chill out in the kitchen and embrace the cooking together thing. Following a recipe is indeed my preferred way of doing things, and I can still do that from time to time. But there is no reason for me to bare my teeth and show the whites of my eyes every time you say, 'Hey babe, have you thought about adding some chilli / salt / lemon to that?'

I also sit on my own a lot. I've noticed that. I put physical distance between us. Which is of course necessary and you don't want someone licking your earlobes or whatever when you are trying to buy a part for your Range Rover online or get through to Belinda / Beatrice at the gas company. But a little more closeness wouldn't go amiss.

Of course the distance from my daughters will always be hard, but if Alistair and I can have the relationship we always intended, then surely the missing them will be less raw. And if I immerse myself totally and utterly in French life, rather than pining for what I left behind, then I will feel more settled, less lonely. Alistair will see how committed I am, we will return to a state of harmony, and then perhaps in a short while my daughters can visit. We have family in the UK and both girls have British passports, so their stay could be extended. It would be so good for them. They could learn Spanish, their grandmother's language, and perhaps spend a year or two in Spain. On the road trip, every time I saw something beautiful, ate something delicious, noticed something comical, I wanted them to be there to experience it too. With Alistair and I living in France, it would make being in Europe so much easier for them, knowing that we were always there as a base to return to if needed.

Going back could secure a future not just for me and Alistair, but for me and my daughters too: this is my reasoning.

———————

The days before I leave are harder than the first time. My younger daughter and I go for a horse trek just north of the city, high in the hills on a tea tree farm overlooking the ocean. It's a family-run horse trek business, and we have visited many times over the years. The owner comes with us as a guide, chatting about the flora and fauna as we go and telling us what it was like growing up on the farm. I remember her some ten years ago, when her mum still ran the business. The daughter has kids of her own now, and they love riding these tracks. *How beautiful*, I think, *that sense of family continuity and togetherness*. The trek is everything I love about New Zealand: the fantails, the native bush, the quiet, the freedom, the privilege of riding this beautiful trail, just the three of us. My daughter is in front of me — her horse's shiny chestnut haunches swaying, its tail flicking — and I can tell she is loving this as much as I am. She turns back and smiles, and it's not the first time over the past few days that I've thought about backing out. But I have promised Alistair, and I have something to prove to myself. None of my relationships have worked out, and perhaps I *am* the common denominator. Perhaps it is me. This time, I want to give it my all.

15

It's Just a Perfect Day

I have decided to say yes to everything. Even to getting back on Alistair's beloved Supermoto 690.

'The nuttiest bastard motorbike that KTM care to make,' is how he fondly describes it, which isn't exactly selling it to me. But I resolve to embrace and participate in Alistair's need for speed — along with every other opportunity that comes my way.

Saying yes to everything may seem like a perilous premise, or even a slightly ovine one. But it's not about being a sheep, or a doormat, or becoming a pathetic adherent of Yes Dear-ism. It's about doing what I came here to do: to get out of my comfort zone. Because my fight for personal sovereignty, during that first seven months with Alistair, did me no good whatsoever. Rather than allowing me to preserve my independence, it only led me to become defensive. To become smaller. I'd become a hostile and suspicious island nation, with Alistair bobbing around in the harbour, increasingly frustrated at not being let in. I don't want a repeat, for my sake or his. Like Sheryl Sandberg and the Tower of Pisa, therefore, I am going to 'lean in'.

I apply this philosophy on my first week back. When Alistair suggests we go for a 'potter' around the locality on the motor-bike, I say 'good idea'. Whether I think this or not is irrelevant. Alistair loves the bike, and so I am going to give it another go. If the terror persists, if I feel that with every lurching acceleration I am going to be tossed into the air like a sad little *crêpe*, I simply won't get on the thing again. You see, I'm not entirely compliant. This 'Let's do it' philosophy comes with a get-out clause. 'Yes' can be readily exchanged for 'hell no' following a full and fair audit of each experience.

So in the mounting heat of this June morning, I don a pair of too-big black jeans, canvas boots, leather jacket and black helmet, which Alistair has me pull on and off so I get the hang of unclipping and clipping it. It's extremely tight, and every time I yank the metallic bulb up past my ears, I sense what a bottle of Dom Pérignon must feel like being uncorked. Alistair has gone for a 'badass-on-holiday-in-Hawaii' look — black biker pants, black Gore-Tex jacket, black helmet and a loud floral shirt. I climb on the back, wrap my arms around his girth and hope for the best.

We judder up the driveway to the road, and I brace myself for the ordeal with a little internal pep talk: *You can do this. Yes, motorbikes are exceedingly dangerous but Alistair is a fantastic rider and knows what he is doing. Yes, he came off the bike last time and could barely walk for two weeks, but to be fair that was on a racetrack. Yes, we have seen a number of tourists driving on the wrong side of the road, and the locals are partial to a lunchtime tipple or three even when they're driving, but really you're safe as houses . . .*

This internal wittering is redundant. Because we are well on our way now, the speed of the bike turning the landscape from fine-detail artwork to blurry impressionism. And I am surprisingly okay. Terror-free. Whether that is because Alistair is going at a mere 100 kilometres per hour when I peep at the clock (as opposed to practically the speed of sound on the previous occasion), or whether my very anticipation of fear has made me resilient to it, I don't know. As we weave through skinny village streets and roar past yellow fields dotted with neatly coiffed haystacks, I'm aware of a new sensation. Could this be, surely not . . . enjoyment? Well, I'll be damned. Insects splatter the visor, which I have to keep nudging up to itch my nose, but apart from this minor discomfort I may just be having fun.

We stop off at the *boulangerie* to buy bread, which I stuff into my backpack. Just a side note here: the *mairie* (town hall) might always be the most imposing building in any French village or town, alongside the church, but the *boulangerie* is arguably the most important one. It is a veritable shrine to the carb where, among the array of baked delights — the glossy flans, fruit-bejewelled tarts, feather-light eclairs and plump *croissants* — the *baguette* is king.

The *baguette* isn't just a stick of bread; it's a way of life. So revered is this culinary staple that in 2022 it was awarded special protection by the UN, with UNESCO granting it Intangible Cultural Heritage status. I'm not exactly sure what this means — whether you might be fined for whacking someone across the head with one, for instance. Or whether it means a *baguette* a day is a basic human right. But I suspect 'protection' means you can't mess too much with the recipe (though I did once see chocolate-flavoured *baguettes* at a Christmas market).

Among the most popular of the myriad varieties on offer are the *baguettes de tradition*. Often made with only flour, water, salt and yeast or leavening, according to tradition they must be baked on site.

I've gone off on a tangent; *excusez-moi*. I blame the *baguettes*.

Next stop is a second-hand clothing market, in full swing in the backyard of a family-run bar. I purchase a black cotton skirt with a lacy hem, a pair of floral shorts (they may be PJ bottoms), two dresses (one a black flapper-style affair with fringey bits) and a striped singlet. All for 2.50 euros. Alistair mistakes the bar proprietor's washing drying on the balcony as another clothing stall and I only just manage to stop him from riffling through a stranger's undies.

We head home for a change of clothes, then stop to eat. It's the seventh birthday of La Boutique d'à Côté, and they've invited customers to a 'little lunch party' on the premises to celebrate. La Boutique d'à Côté (literally 'the shop next door') is open only on a Saturday until around 1 p.m., selling wine and food crafted by some 40 local producers. Alistair insists we get there early, before the 'little French ladies with sharp elbows' get all the best stuff. But it's not at all feral really; if anything the atmosphere is genteel and convivial.

Alistair's favourite product is Jerusalem artichoke purée, which he's taken to adding to everything, including beef *bourguignon* (he's a 'wing-it' kind of cook and swears this gives the sauce extra oomph). He proudly passes this culinary tip onto the chap at the checkout, who smiles but leans forward to say: 'Perhaps don't try that in Burgundy (the home of *bourguignon*).'

A repository of *bonhomie* and community spirit, the store is everything you'd hope to find in a French village. Here among the celeriac and the pestos, the bottles of golden saffron and craft beers, the organic wines and artisan cheeses, you'll bump into the lady from the post office, the local librarian, the neighbours, other store owners, the mayor, the plumber. People stop to chat in the rather restricted space, something we found annoying at first then realised that this happy chitter-chatter only goes to show the venue is meeting its original brief as a 'community glue'.

Founded and run by volunteers, the store was the brainchild of a group of locals who wanted to give a hand-up to the region's producers, showcase local art and culture, and foster a little social cohesion. A former upholsterer's workshop that had lain empty for years, the dilapidated property was virtually rebuilt from scratch by this enthusiastic team. They exposed the beautiful stonework, replaced the floor and roof, put in new electricity and plumbing and turned it into the quaint little store–social hub it is today.

Another side note (and honestly, feel free to shimmy right on past it into the courtyard, where they're now serving *apéritifs*. I'll be along in a minute).

When I first encountered the shop, I was almost disappointed. We'd been told there was an amazing artisan produce store and in my mind it would be something bigger, brighter, more picturesque. I'd expected chintzy interior-design flourishes, more products, chirpy staff in crisp aprons and perhaps a jauntily placed hay bale or two. So accustomed had I become to the fake rustic vibe of many an urban deli, I was underwhelmed by the real thing. I read the nonchalance of the store attendants as a lack of commitment or even boredom. Now that I know a little of the shop's origins, I see it all for what it really is. A collection of quality products that don't need to shout to be appreciated. And a gathering of generous and humble local producers and volunteers whose low-key delivery isn't indifference — it's humility and a quiet pride in what has been achieved here.

In the courtyard next to the store, a long table is laden with what I take to be our lunch. But it's just the warm-up act. A white tablecloth is the canvas for a culinary artwork of breads, pestos made with fennel and sunflower seeds, slices of spicy *chorizo*, *prosciutto*-style hams, goat's cheese, olives, pork *rillettes* and more. One of the shop's founders, Claude, serves us big plastic cups of knock-your-socks-off punch that tastes of lollies but sets my head on a fast spin cycle.

I chat to a diminutive elderly lady called Camille who has short silver hair and a face that radiates warmth and benevolence like a good fairy. Camille also deserves a Pulitzer Prize in Journalism for 'Extracting the Most Information from an Interviewee in the Shortest Time'.

Her manner is so gently inquisitive, however, that I'm flattered rather than offended. What might have felt like an interrogation is softened by empathetic nods and interjections — and the fact she is genuinely curious and not trying to meet a newspaper deadline. 'How long have you been here? Where are you living? Oh, a *moulin*! How charming! Oh, that's Alistair? He has a nice face. Does he own the *moulin*? I love to be by a river. Where did you meet? How did you meet? Ah, online dating. It's the only way these days, isn't it — how else are you meant to find someone? Will you stay? Ah yes, it's hard to be away from family. What do your daughters think? What do they do? You must be so proud . . . Will they come and visit you?'

When I try to explain to her what it is I love about France, I find myself unable to distil the sentiment so instead gesture to everything around me. 'Oh yes,' she replies. 'The French have mastered *l'art de vivre*.' Precisely.

Lovely as Camille is, I need to stop talking. My brain is putting up a 'closed for lunch' sign. Because even ten minutes is a hell of a long time to chat in a language that's not your own. And the glass of rocket-fuel punch hasn't helped. Searching for vocabulary and noun endings, I'm like a drunk trying to find his keys. So I make my excuses and bury myself in the crowd, eager to lose myself for a few minutes, to be a mere unit of humanity rather than a person with a long and complicated back story.

The understatement of the store isn't echoed here. This is a birthday party with bells on. There's an accordion player, and a couple of clowns, and a sensational trio of mature gentlemen in bowler hats playing jazz and swing and generally bringing the celebratory vibe. Later on there will be an open mic for poetry, singing or whatever people feel brave enough (or have had enough punch, beer and wine) to attempt.

Unsurprisingly, the lunch menu consists only of meat and I find myself nonsensically wondering which is the most vegetarian out of 'pork, lamb or beef'. 'Well just eat the coleslaw and potatoes,' says Alistair, with maddening logic. I shoot him a look that (I hope) says 'Would *you* be happy with coleslaw and potatoes?' and order the beef. After all, it would be rude to spurn the regional produce.

We sit at a table with a local performer who runs clown courses, his girlfriend who works at the village retirement home and another young couple whom we never get to know because we can't hear each other above the music. Our relationship is limited to smiling and raising glasses.

After a hectic three-and-a-half hours I'm done. We've eaten, drunk, talked, laughed, drunk and eaten some more, and even danced.

I also appear to have signed up for a clown workshop.

———

It's taken me most of a lifetime to understand what being an introvert really means. It may manifest differently in some individuals, but for me it means I can love people, be energised by their company and do a passable impersonation of bubbliness. But when I'm over it, I'm over it.

Drained of battery, I'm irretrievable, and no amount of yelling into me works. I'm unmoved by exhortations like 'We can't go *now*! We're having so much fun!!' I just want to go home, and preferably be left alone with a cup of tea. However sometimes, so as not to cramp my companions' style, I agree to hang around a bit longer. I get through by nodding and smiling enthusiastically so people don't notice that I've emotionally checked out. Though they really shouldn't fail to notice, because this version of me is vastly inferior to my fully charged self, due to far fewer working features and patchy reception.

Today is a perfect example of my introversion kicking in. After hours of chatting and eating and smiling — much of it in French (the chatting, not the smiling) — my jaws hurt, my brain hurts, my personality hurts, my feet hurt and I want to go home. Luckily so does Alistair. And luckily he shares my opinion that after a day of heat and hedonism, what's needed first is a siesta (we sleep on the sofa for over two hours), then an evening jaunt on the e-bikes. Fresh air, no alcohol, and only scenery on the menu.

It's around 8.30 p.m. when we set off on the bikes and, as we clock up the kilometres, I start to feel at peace. The honeyed evening light, the faint breeze, my conscientious legs pedalling away all the excesses of the boozy lunch . . . I'm renewed, refreshed. And, if my body is still more liquor store than temple, the seedy feeling is giving way to a great sense of wellbeing. I don't care that I am wearing my 50-*centime* stripey top with no bra, some teensy-tiny hand-me-down shorts, that my hair is plastered to my sweaty face, my eyeliner smeared, my legs bristly and pasty from months of New Zealand rain. I'm okay with all of it.

Until we enter the town square.

There are people everywhere. The village square is usually dead at night, something I've often lamented but think longingly of right now. It's as if all the people from lunch have simply swayed across the street, bought beer, sat down and then phoned all our neighbours to join them.

There are food trucks and beverage trucks and the air smells of candy floss and cooking oil. There are people on chairs and sitting at the base of statues, there are clusters of friends laughing and smoking and talking, and children running everywhere. There is a man with long grey hair with a dirty growl of a voice singing into a mic under a gazebo. He seems oddly out of place at this family event, like Serge Gainsbourg at a four-year-old's birthday party.

Having not been reunited with friends since I returned, I don't want to see them while I'm like this. I'm tired, sweaty and, minus the big floppy hat, dressed like Jodie Foster in *Taxi Driver* (teen prostitute, if you haven't seen it). I remain steadfastly straddled across my bike as Alistair dismounts and heads over to a gaggle of familiar faces in the distance. If I keep staring at my handlebars,

Alistair will get the message, we will cycle home and nobody will ever know I am capable of looking like this.

But no. After some five minutes I look up and he is gesturing wildly. People are waving so I wave back and wonder how long this waving can continue without me actually making a move in their direction. Eventually I schlepp over, prop up the bike and go to greet them. There are many kisses, hugs, expressions of delight and some gentle back-slapping. Our next-door-neighbour Gabriel is there in an instant, offering to shout us a beer. I glare at Alistair in an 'Erm, please no,' way but instantly feel cruel as he's clearly delighted to be here. Remembering my vow to just say yes, I tell Gabriel, 'Sure, thank you.'

Alistair looks relieved. He leans towards me and whispers reassuringly, 'It's fine. You're fine. Besides, nobody here cares. They're not like that. They're just really genuine people and they're not going to judge you.'

The long-haired singer isn't quitting. His lyrics contain a lot of swearing and now he's in the middle of a gritty ditty about the 'HLM' — social housing. It's bizarre and anachronistic, especially when a couple start slow-dancing to it. Gabriel says, 'That guy is famous. Or wait, no . . . maybe he just looks like someone famous.'

The thing is, Alistair is right. Nobody cares. They don't care whether this guy once had a Top 40 hit or is just an obscure lookalike. They don't care about my tiny orange shorts, or that the only food is burgers and hot dogs, or that the kids will be cranky in the morning after too much sugar and too little sleep. They don't care that not a vegetable has passed their lips all day, that they haven't drunk their recommended quota of water, that they're not wearing their best frocks, or that they are due for a haircut. They are here for a good time, to celebrate being together with family and friends on this glorious Saturday evening, and that's all there is to it. Perhaps they instinctively know something I am only just realising. That things don't have to be flawless to be perfect.

So I get out of my own way, take a deep breath of the fried food-infused night air, and settle in. We spend two hours with our friends then cycle home in the darkness.

As we arrive at the mill, I gaze up at the moon: a perfectly round, shimmering full stop to a perfectly wonderful day.

16

Fireworks

Alistair and I are lounging. It's 9.45 p.m. and we're draped — Dali melted clock-fashion — over the furniture. We've just eaten a late and rather weird dinner, which is the only kind served at the *moulin*. We're big on finishing up stuff, Alistair more so than me. I draw the line at furry cheese.

Tonight it was *haricots verts*, pine nuts, pumpkin seeds, carrots and spring onions — all tossed together with questionable bits of *prosciutto* and a vinaigrette of indeterminate use-by date (I can't recall when I made it). In a 'Why not?' moment we threw a fried egg on top. And of course there was the compulsory *baguette* and glass of red.

Tonight is 13 July, i.e. the day before 14 July (bear with me). The significance of this is that 14 July is Bastille Day, as it's known everywhere except France, where it's simply *'la fête nationale'*.

The day celebrates the storming of the Bastille prison by the people of Paris in 1789, an act which signalled the start of the French Revolution. A French friend told us, 'You know, there were only a handful of prisoners in there when the people fought their way in. But that is not the point — it's the symbolism of it! These were political prisoners!' He said this with great passion.

On the eve of this public holiday everyone goes to town (villages included) by letting off fireworks. Tonight's public display is at 11 p.m., which is a challenge given our current state of dynamism. I'm all for sloping off to bed with my book, but it would be a shame to miss out on this calendar highlight. So we agree to head out by bike, in the certainty that the night air and dicing with traffic in the pitch black will soon wake us up.

I stay close behind Alistair on the road, as my headlamp doesn't work too well. At one point I have problems shifting gears, panic as a car approaches from behind, wobble off onto the verge and have to head back the way we came, downhill. I can't re-mount on an incline. 'What the *hell* are you doing?' says Alistair when I catch up with him. I can't tell him because I am laughing too much.

————

Forty-five years ago, to the day. That's when I last gazed up at the Bastille Day fireworks.

The year was 1977, and I stood on a river bank in a Parisian suburb with Françoise and Thierry, the couple I was nannying for. With us were their two children: little Cyril, a blond, cherubic nightmare, and skinny Lionel, impish and adorable. Lionel had unruly dark hair, a pinched face, slightly sticky-out top teeth and pencil-sharp shoulder blades. There was something urchin-like about him, despite his growing up in a middle-class Parisian postcode. I much preferred his raggle-taggle naughtiness to the slightly mummy's boy entitlement of Cyril (give him a break, Maria, he was only four. At that stage in my life, however, I didn't have time for children and planned to never have any of my own). We watched the sky spit out sparks and erupt into flame, and laughed that the oscillating reflection of a train crossing the bridge was prettier than the display.

Nineteen. I had no idea what was to come. I didn't know that my then-worst nightmare (having a Cyril and Lionel of my own) would be the source of my greatest joy. That I would live for many more decades (the nuclear arms race was revving up and even the next week didn't seem guaranteed). That I would get my modern languages degree, that my father would die of a heart attack in four years' time, that I would leave everyone I loved to live on the other side of the world — and do it all again in the opposite direction. That I would be deliriously happy, heartbroken, extremely poor and have everything I dreamt of and more.

This current firework display is beyond beautiful. I'm crying now, and in solidarity a cascade of sparks ripples down from each viaduct arch.

How did it happen? I mean, seriously what the hell? How was I nineteen one moment, and 64 the next? It's like I nipped off to buy ice cream and returned to find a thief had made off with an entire Parisian family and four decades of my life.

I share this with Alistair. 'Yep, it all goes so fast. I guess the big question is, would you do anything differently?'

I stare at the red flares bursting from the bridge. No regrets, that's always been my mantra. But mantras are mantras. They're not the truth. So many wrong turns, bad choices, batshit moves, terrible relationships. Then I think of my two daughters.

'Not a thing,' I reply.

17

Le Mans

As promised in my 'manifesto' to Alistair, I make an effort to throw myself headlong into French life. I start a weekly stint of volunteering, make moves to join a tennis club, and investigate local horse treks rather than longing for the tea tree trail back home. With little money, I don't actually do any of the paid activities, but at least I am laying down the foundations for when I can. Calling in randomly on the neighbours still feels too uncomfortable, but I do try to say 'Yes!' to all the adventures Alistair throws my way.

The first one is a trip to the motorsport event 24 Hours of Le Mans. Alistair is extremely excited about this. Unlike the prelude to the Spain roadie, he doesn't need my enthusiasm to match his. His million-megawatt zeal carries us both. And while cars aren't really my thing, I am intrigued by the prospect of attending this world-famous event. Even I recognise that this is an exceptional opportunity. It is not just the annual classic car race; the 2023 extravaganza will mark 100 years since the very first one was held, with some of the original Bentleys even competing, and more than 800 cars will take part over four days.

Arriving in Le Mans after an almost three-hour drive, we join thousands of others camping at the public campsite next to the circuit. In this field crammed with motorhomes, caravans and pop-up tents is the most divine array of cars. Classic Porsches are parked beside modest nylon shelters. Sleek Jaguar D-Types crouch low next to plastic picnic tables. AC Cobras bristle with unleashed energy next to barbecues and chilly bins.

When we first arrive at the ground, a man on a bicycle tells us to follow him, so he can show us to our camping spot. He stops next to a corner site, says something, indicates, then pedals off again up the muddy path. After a good 40 minutes putting up our tent in increasingly persistent rain, a second man on a pushbike brakes to a halt next to us. 'Can't camp there!' he says brightly. 'That's for the first aid station!' Alistair and I look at each other, but by now we are so tired, so wet, and so uncomfortable that the situation has morphed into comedy. I wipe the rain out of my eyes, remind Alistair of the cold beer that comes at the end of this, and start to pull up pegs.

———————

Le Mans is memorable, for many reasons. The races themselves are of little interest because I have no emotional connection to any of it; I'm not rooting for any driver in particular, I'm not aware of who the underdogs, the courageous veterans, nor who the surprise comebacks are. All of those elements that add spice to watching a sport are missing for me. My fault entirely, of course, but I merely mention it.

However, I do love to learn about the characters who have taken part over the decades. Running along one long fence by the track is a display of photographs, accompanied by narrative, of Le Mans over the past 100 years. The one which charms me most is a fuzzy 1969 colour image of drivers running across the track at the start of the race. That was the tradition; the moment the starting flag came down, competitors sprinted to their cars and often didn't take the time to belt up, so eager were they to get ahead of the field. Every driver in that photo is running, but one. Racing icon Jacky Ickx is pictured strolling to his car, staging a one-man protest at the dangerous sprinting tradition. When he got to the car, the story goes, he made a show of slowly and carefully doing up his belts in order to press home his point. Ickx was proved right, in the most tragic of ways. A fellow competitor that day, John Woolfe, sped off unbuckled, lost control of his car, crashed into the barriers and died after being flung from the cockpit. Ickx, meanwhile, won the race.

———————

There's a lot to love about Le Mans, even for the non-petrol-heads among us. It looks, feels, sounds and smells like one long celebration. Delicious aromas waft from the many food trucks, the *al fresco* bars and restaurants are packed with clientele of all kinds sipping cold beers and *champagne* in the sunshine; music blares from speakers and as you walk, the warbling of Édith Piaf gives way to a burst of samba, which further along gives way to the thudding of a rock ballad. There is entertainment for kids, while stalls — some tiny, some lavish — sell everything from posters and branded baseball caps to leather racing suits and, yes, actual cars. Once I have stopped bristling at the very idea of it all, i.e. the decidedly pungent whiff of privilege in the air, I begin to focus on other things. Like the genius and passion that goes into creating these glorious machines, the bravery and sheer determination of the drivers, the heart-warming dedication of the fans. I see an elderly man collecting autographs from the drivers, his face shining like the boy he once was as he approaches, pen in hand.

We're inside a non-stop theme park, reality on pause for four days. Apart from one afternoon, when the outside world comes to us loud and clear over an intercom: a reminder to anyone who needs to take public transport that trains will not be running after 8.15 p.m. Because beyond these gates, France is burning. Two days ago, after the shooting at point-blank range of a teenager of Moroccan–Algerian descent in Nanterre, the streets began to pour with justifiable rage at the killing. The flames of fury show no sign of dying down. In multiple cities from north to south, cars and public buildings are set ablaze. There is rioting and looting. Many are expressing shock and outrage at this behaviour. But others, like French journalist Rokhaya Diallo writing in *The Washington Post*, beautifully lay out why it should shock no one.

> If the world seems to be astonished by the level of anger expressed, I am not. France has been facing police brutality against minorities for decades, a problem that lingers and worsens with time. If the status quo is left unchecked, if this systemic racist violence continues apace, a proudly 'universalist' republic — and especially one that purports not to recognize racial, religious, or ethnic difference at all — will have abandoned its own social contract.

———————

On the last night, when Le Mans is winding down, we return to the campsite. It is empty. The sleek beasts have evacuated the savannah, the makeshift homes have been pulled up, rolled up and ferried out. There remain one or two dotted here and there. And amusingly, the tent right next to ours is one of them. A whole vacant field and two little tents pressed up close to each other, as if scared to be alone. Our neighbours are a father and son who come to Le Mans together every year. They offer us *sangria* and we chat to them for a good hour before saying goodnight, climbing into the tent, and zipping another day closed.

The next morning, we wake early, around 6.30, and dismantle the tent — again in the pouring rain. My shorts are drenched, but I tell myself, 'No matter, we will soon be sitting in a cosy café drinking coffee and eating *pain au chocolat*'. We set off and, heading out of Le Mans, Alistair remarks that the Range Rover is low on petrol. He's not too worried about it; there is still enough fuel to get us to a service station he sees marked on the map. But the fuel gauge is giving us fake news. 'Oh shit,' says Alistair, with the gravitas that tells you this is not an overreaction to something minor, like he's just remembered he left the milk out of the fridge back home. The car starts to slow. With some bizarre but clever steering-wheel handling, Alistair manages to coax it onto a grass verge, right before a set of traffic lights and in the middle of two dual carriageways. We are just coming into a small town, but it's 8 a.m. and nothing is open. The fuel station we were destined for is a good three kilometres away. We sit, not talking, just waiting — as if the car is simply having a bad episode and will get up and start moving again when it has taken a few deep breaths. In this pause of uncertainty, I take time to savour the irony that we've run out of fuel mere minutes from one of the world's most famous racetracks. Finally, I say 'Look, why don't I walk to the petrol station, and bring back fuel in a thingy.' 'A canister,' says Alistair. 'And thank you. You are amazing.' He has had a bad back for days now, so I am not amazing. I am in fact the only shortlisted candidate.

What follows is a French farce of Feydeau-esque proportions. Alistair hands me a bunch of cash so I can buy the petrol. It has to be E95, he reminds me. I set off and walk. And walk. And walk some more. Low on fuel myself, I am highly tempted to go off-*piste* in search of a bakery, but I have a mission to complete and I can't leave Alistair on his grass atoll in the midst of a sea of traffic. Finally, after a good 25 minutes or more, I spy the gas station. I am drenched and starving and cold, and I must be a pitiful sight. Which is probably why, when I explain my dilemma, the attendant nips out the back and returns with an empty plastic canister — see-through like a milk bottle — which she doesn't charge me for. I head out to the forecourt, happy to spot an E95 sign. Then another attendant, just arriving, yells out, 'You can't take away fuel in that! It's illegal!' I protest that her co-worker only just gave me the thing. She shrugs. 'Up to you,' she says, in a 'I wash my hands of you' tone. 'But if you get stopped . . .'

The automatic-pay machine at the pump doesn't take cash. It's the only E95 pump here. I have Alistair's card, but no pin number. I try to call him, but remember his phone is flat and, with the car not working, he can't recharge it. I try unsuccessfully to persuade the attendant to take my cash for the E95, but no. Eventually, she offers up the fact: 'That pump over there takes cash.' It does, but it doesn't dispense E95. Unable to get hold of Alistair, I figure that any fuel is better than no fuel. And even if this does give the Rangie indigestion, it's going to get us far enough to fill up on the good stuff. I pay up and trudge the three kilometres back in the pouring rain, my several litres of illegality sloshing around in its plastic container. Quite honestly, if I were a *flic* (cop), I'd arrest me right now. In the midst of nationwide riots where arson is a go-to expression of discontent and loathing, a small damp person in a hoodie who looks like she slept the night in an aquarium is moving darkly along the streets, carrying several litres of incriminating liquid. So, in a very un-Le Mans racetrack kind of way, this petrol is facilitating a burst of speed, leading me to walk faster and faster, finding a gear I didn't even know I had.

I make it back to the car, tired, hungry but with my liberty intact — having passed no cops along the way. Alistair can't believe it. He assumed I would get lost, give up, and come back angry and frustrated. But no, here I am, dripping with rain and satisfaction. He gives me the biggest hug. 'You are amazing,' he says. And this time, yes I am.

18

Drowning and Surfacing

Alistair loves the river. Maybe because he *is* the river. Dynamic, invigorating, with an unstoppable momentum that can leave you in awe.

It's not just me who recognises this. I hear this first-hand from his mates too. One Friday, a cluster of them — long-time motorcycling buddies from the UK — come to spend a weekend. Over dinner at the local pizza place that night, the three guys mention they have a WhatsApp group chat titled 'What Would Alistair Do?' Alistair didn't know about this but is visibly flattered. I ask why, and as an example they cite a motorcycle trip incident in Europe a few years back. They turned up late on their bikes for a ferry crossing and, seeing the ship about to depart, resigned themselves to waiting for the next one, if there was a next one. But Alistair wasn't having it. With a yelled 'Come on!' he roared off in the direction of the boat, racing up onto the car ramp seconds before it was raised. Stunned, they sped after him, and made it by a whisker.

It's all very amusing and I tease him about his James Bond aspirations. But there's also a side to this 'man of action' persona that unnerves me. Alistair is a force. A force, as I mentioned earlier, he himself is unaware of. His energy is immense; it could power five water mills. His love for me is overwhelming — it has a vigour that threatens to knock me off my feet, as if I'm standing in the current by the water mill's penstock. And the absence of it . . . well, that has a potency all of its own.

When Alistair is not pleased, you know for sure he's not pleased. The air crackles with it. When he is in a mood, it's like a door slamming shut. He's not an actual door-slammer, but he might as well be. There's a sense of something severed, something leaving the room. Love was here, and now it's not. It feels wholesale — not 'Alistair loves me but right now he is angry', more like 'Alistair loved me five minutes ago and now he doesn't.' Oh I get it. I know this is my stuff talking too. But believe me, when it feels like it's happening, it's devastating. Like that moment just as you are falling asleep when you suddenly wake with a lurch in your guts. It's like that.

It's a curious thing, to embark on an adventure, to hurl yourself headlong into it — to tell the world and yourself, 'Look at *me* throwing caution and postcodes to the wind! Look at *me*, a little carefree thistledown, blowing through the vast emptiness of uncertainty.' Only to realise, when you feel love ebbing and flowing, that there is one thing which you crave above all others. Security.

These episodes where Alistair and I detach from one another, they shake me to the core. Why the ebbing and flowing? If I knew that, instead of this book I would be writing one called *How to Stop Your Relationship from Capsizing and Other Terrible Nautical Metaphors*. All I can say is this. Deep wounds make people act in unhelpful ways. And I mean this for both me and Alistair.

I am to learn that Alistair finds I am often aloof and my distance makes him anxious. My behaviour speaks to his deepest fears. Not knowing what to do with that, he turns within.

And my own fear of rejection, my terror of yet another relationship falling apart, make me interpret this withdrawal as the beginning of the end. It fuels my sense of isolation, and turns me into a small, frightened animal. A more resilient Maria would go to him, understand he needs nurture, not conflict. Being scared is making me unempathetic. But I feel emotionally unsafe. Here, in a place with no personal history to ground me, with few reminders of who I really am — only Alistair's displeasure to reflect back at me a Maria who is uncaring, unkind and hard to live with — I am honestly not the 'best version of myself', as they say.

Financial insecurity is only fanning the flames. In Auckland, while I was never prosperous, I always just about managed to keep my head above water. I was resourceful and proud of my self-reliance. Now however, I am in trouble. Soon after I arrive back at Alistair's, my freelance work starts drying up, which seems like the universe's tasteless little prank. Because it has never been an issue before; I am usually turning jobs down. Technical difficulties only make the little work that I do have extremely challenging. The wifi fades in and out, I can't access the servers I need, and let's just say I start to get extremely agitated. Alistair tells me, 'Hey don't worry . . . you've got me to look after you.' He sees 'providing for me' as his job; he's old-fashioned like that. This makes me recoil. Partly because I am more independent than I knew. But also because, like the dodgy wifi, our connection is not stable. Sometimes I say outright, 'Alistair, we fight too much. You say you'll look after me . . . but what about when you don't want to anymore?' This hurts him; it presses on more bruises that I don't know the origin of.

You can see what is happening here. Two people who desperately need kindness, and desperately need it from each other, are retreating to their own corners to lick their sores and pick at their scabs, before returning for another bout in the ring. The sense of distance from what we promised ourselves, the disconnect with the marketing material — the Greatest Love Affair Ever! Never Too Late to Find the One! — only highlights the disappointment. This was intended to be a masterpiece; it was never meant to have serious flaws. Of course this is not how it is all the time. Relationships persist, keep stumbling forwards, because they are rarely made solely of pain. In between the hard moments are great shafts of light that make you believe again.

19

Visa Day

I have been summoned.

When you are going through the morass of paperwork to apply for your French *carte de séjour* (residence permit), you can think of no happier state than being a legal long-stay visa holder. I imagined it like a 'before and after' — 'before' you are nothing but Brexit McBrexit Face, a sad loser who must keep her eye on the calendar for fear of overstaying. 'After', you are a daughter of the Republic, embraced and kissed on both cheeks by the French state, free to frolic unhindered to the 90-day point and beyond. But in fact . . . not so fast. There are a number of post-visa formalities to comply with. First and most important, the requirement that you validate your visa soon after returning to France, otherwise it doesn't count. That's easily enough done online. But then you have to attend a series of 'induction days' — I suppose to show you take it all seriously, that you are as committed to *égalité, fraternité* and *liberté* as the next chap. These are compulsory; if you don't attend you jeopardise your chance of extending the visa.

While I was in New Zealand for that four-month holiday, I received a letter requesting my presence for the first of these steps: a medical followed by a morning of language assessments and an introduction to French life. Of course I had to reschedule.

That's how one Wednesday, three weeks after my return and a full nine months after getting my visa, I have a date at the nearest hospital for the pre-medical lung X-ray. The X-ray is to screen for tuberculosis, which strikes me as a tad 'the horse has bolted'. If I do have TB, my lungs will have been innards *non grata* for quite some time.

In all honesty, I doubt that I am carrying this or any other undesirable stowaways in the lung department. What I am nervous about, however, is the language tests. How embarrassing, if the woman with an Honours degree in French falls at this hurdle. Alistair kindly tracks down some sample exams online, and after 40 minutes of having a crack at these writing and comprehension tests, my confidence is restored. Even if I fail on the day, I now know for certain that I can pen 60 words about my best friend, and chat knowledgeably about the shamefully low supply of early childcare in suburban Paris. If I ever get stuck for something to talk about at a social gathering, I will steer the conversation around to bosom pals or the problems facing young families in the capital.

The X-ray and the tests are to take place on two consecutive days. So rather than make the two-hour round trip twice, we opt to stay overnight at an Airbnb in the town centre. A music festival is on at the same time, with live bands and performers in the squares and many of the bars, so it seems like ideal timing.

On the day of the X-ray, Alistair and I are both flustered. We are running late, and being late and flustered translates into a modicum of tetchiness. 'So what's the address?' asks Alistair as we get into the Berlingo, in a tone that says, 'You haven't bothered to look up the address, have you?' As I fumble around with maps on my phone, he starts to get snappy and I start to feel unbalanced. It's the usual chain reaction: Disorganised Maria + Combustible Alistair = Upset Maria and 20 Minutes of Discord. It's marvellous really, how reliable this formula is. I wish I'd been taught this in O Level Chemistry.

The argument is futile, because we do make it to the hospital on time. Once the X-ray is completed, we head into town for lunch then spend a pleasant afternoon just strolling through the pretty historic streets.

———————————

That night is warm and sultry, and we choose a restaurant for its outside tables and live performance by a talented guitarist. He is nothing if not versatile, belting out everything from The Beatles to popular French ballads. But the real crowd-pleasers are his Disney songs, astonishing given that the audience is made up entirely of inebriated adults. The rousing reception to 'Let it Go' is indicative; we have indeed let it go, all our inhibitions drowned in a vat of Aperol spritzes and *prosecco*. We linger for several hours and totter back gingerly along some very narrow footpaths.

It's stifling inside our accommodation, so we open the Velux skylight to feel the air on our faces. There is none; instead it's like someone has thrown a warm towel over our heads. Thanks to too much Aperol and wine, the stultifying heat and a tremendous storm, I toss and turn and am awake most of the night. In the morning, we discover the rain has poured in through the skylight, all over the carpet and into our overnight bags. Every single item of clothing is sodden. After several frantic minutes of hairdryer treatment, the clothes have progressed from properly drenched to mildly wet.

When Alistair drops me off at the offices for 'immigration and integration' for a morning of French assessments I am so damp, hungover and sleep-deprived I doubt I would pass a test in my own language.

————

For the first hour, my fellow immigrants and I are left to complete a multiple-choice questionnaire and a writing assessment. My brain cells stretch and yawn, but once they begin to wake up, the whole thing is surprisingly pain-free. Enjoyable even. One by one we are called into a side room for a 'chat', i.e. an oral language test. While we wait, a video plays on the big screen in front of us, explaining France's values, what is expected of us, and what our rights are. The video is short, and plays repeatedly on a loop. In one section, we are told 'In France you can do whatever you like and be whoever you want, as long as it is within the law' and the irony is not lost on me that dispensing with the law — i.e. revolution — is what modern France is built on.

When it's my turn for the assessment, I sit opposite a cheery young woman whose first question is 'So what brought you here?' When I tell her I came for love and that I live in a romantic mill by a river, she becomes quite animated. After a few minutes, it's hard to tell whether she is still asking questions to gauge my use of prepositions and pronouns or whether this has now slipped into genuine curiosity. Reflecting sadly that many of the immigrants who come through here are fleeing war or political persecution, I suppose that my frivolous story is a welcome spot of light relief.

At the end of the chat, my interlocutor smiles brightly and says 'Your French is VERY good!' then explains that because of this, it's entirely optional whether I take their free, month-long advanced language course. As this would require me driving an hour every day, I decline. But I'm impressed that the reason for the tests is not to weed people out, simply to help in your French learning journey by assessing your level and offering further study if needed.

Finally, the medical. It's not an actual medical, just a revision of my lung X-ray. Knowing this is the last step in the process, I breathe easy. In a cramped office, an elderly doctor in a white coat sits behind a desk. The white coat is a nice touch, if a bit excessive given that he is merely assessing bits of paper. The doctor chats non-stop, barely looking at me. He mentions orange juice several times, I am not sure why. Partly because I am not listening. I have become distracted by the way he is frowning at my X-ray. He looks up. 'Do you smoke?' he asks. 'Oh no,' I tell him. 'I used to, but I stopped just before I had children.' He nods in approval.

'Well,' he goes on. 'You have a mark, just here, on your X-ray. Have you seen this before?'

I lean over and see a small blob of white on one rib, which looks like not much to me. Tiredness has taken over again, and I feel almost giggly. I want to suggest it might be a *baguette* crumb.

'It could be nothing,' he says. 'It could have been there for years. But since you don't know that for sure, and we don't know whether it's on your actual lung or on the bone, you will need to follow this up.'

He shouldn't really approve my medical, he says, but he will. As long as I promise to get the mark investigated as soon as I can.

On the bright side, I don't have TB.

———

'Bonjour messieurs/dames.'

Another patient takes their seat in the waiting room. The French are incredibly civil like this. Always when you enter a small enough venue — be it a *boulangerie*, a GP's clinic like this one, a café — you greet those already there. On the street, too,

205

when you pass total strangers, the custom is to say *'Bonjour!'* It's a lovely way of being acknowledged. You're not just a bunch of randoms forced to share a space but individuals who deserve a greeting.

As I wait for Danielle the doctor to look at my X-ray and refer me for an MRI, I study a poster on the wall about safe drinking. No more than two small glasses of wine a day, it cautions. And at least two days alcohol-free a week. This makes me smile. Maybe it's the rustic life, but I know few people here who would stick to that. It should really say, 'No more than two glasses of wine before lunch.' Alcohol is everywhere. It's partly that *art de vivre*, where every occasion is one to embrace. Pop round to a neighbour at any hour of the day and they will offer you *un petit café*, a beer, wine or an *apéro*. The latter always sounds innocent enough but often involves an extremely strong Ricard or two along with an array of snacks.

Drinks are frequent, and often unexpected. As part of the village *fête*, there is always a *randonnée* (trek) of around five kilometres on the Sunday morning. It's not an arduous walk, just a social affair really. Alistair and I went last year, and it was a beautiful stroll along dappled paths and beside the river. After walking for about half an hour, we turned a corner to see our neighbour Antoine with his little beach buggy, parked at the side of the track. In the back was a hot coffee dispenser, trays of pastries, some fruit and of course wine. 'It's 10.30 a.m.,' I said to Alistair. 'And we have walked two and a half kilometres.' When I express the same surprise to Antoine, he looks at me baffled.

He just glances at his watch, as if worried he might have been late with the wine, and nods.

So back to the doctor's. I'm snapped out of my musings about alcohol by Danielle calling me into her clinic. During our consultation, she peers at the X-ray and says rather matter-of-factly, 'It's not necessarily cancer.' That makes me jump. Partly because I hadn't thought it was necessarily anything of the kind, and partly at her directness. As she hands me my hospital referral, she looks up and smiles. 'Your French is very good!' she says brightly. Lovely of her to comment. Though honestly? I'd far rather people were praising the glowing health of my organs rather than my linguistic skills.

20

More Fireworks

Alistair and I have the mother of all fights, outside the *moulin* one evening. We are supposed to be going to a party, and I have made it as far as sitting in the front seat of the Deuche. In a new white dress, heels, make-up, newly washed hair, perfume even, I am ready. What I am not prepared for is the argument that erupts. I should have been. Alistair has been on a low simmer all day, because of something unrelated to me, but now he's fully on the boil. The yellow Citroën has become an angry saucepan, and the lid is about to start rattling with the pressure of the steam.

As is the way with relationships, the immediate topic of debate isn't the real issue. What does matter is that Alistair speaks to me coldly, I get triggered, then angry, then Alistair gets mad, then I get out of the car (with the must-have slam of the door), there is shouting, and he drives away. For all I know, he's gone for the night. On the most perfect of summer evenings, when the sun pours down like honey (thank you Leonard Cohen), in a setting made for romance . . . I am left standing alone. I have no money, no keys to the locked house, and no car keys. Everyone appears to be out or on holiday so I can't even take my party-ready self to the neighbours for a pick-me-up and a calm down. Instead I am forced to clamber into the *moulin* by a first-floor window, in a little white dress. When I say 'forced', I mean it's the only productive channel for my fury. I first have to heave a steel ladder eight times my height and weight from the barn down a series of stone steps and prop it beneath the window. It is a feat of determination and strength that leaves me frankly astonished and Alistair, as he later admits, highly impressed. Once inside the mill, I book a plane ticket to London and pack my case much like I am stuffing information into this paragraph — chaotically, inadequately and leaving more questions than answers.

Alistair returns after an hour and is surprised to see me doing things to a suitcase that would give Marie Kondo conniptions. But I insist; I am not staying.

Leaving the country after a tiff may seem like an overreaction; and let's face it, a walk around the block would be a lot cheaper. However, I am so angry and upset that I need to get away for a decent chunk of time. And I don't yet know anyone well enough in the village to turn up on their doorstep requesting asylum. I need time to think. It can't go on like this; our arguments just seem to be getting progressively bigger and louder.

Over the next two weeks, staying with my brother and sister-in-law in a leafy (aka posh) west London suburb, I have plenty of space to reflect. They are immensely kind and nurturing and astonishingly non-judgmental. Not an eyeroll in sight — which is remarkable given they've seen the Maria Heartache Show before, several times. Kept the programme, bought the poster, got the T-shirt. Instead of lecturing, they whisk me away for a weekend to their holiday home in idyllic Dorset. We walk to the pub along a narrow pathway cut through a field of towering corn — shimmering and golden in the evening light. We eat hot Cornish pasties, laze on the beach, attend a village-wide hat competition (a woman with a home-made plastic aquarium on her head deservedly takes first prize), listen to live street music and generally bask in feel-good holiday vibes. Back in London, I take Guinness for long walks around Richmond Park. A dog is ideal live-in-the-moment therapy — we scamper along together, playing ball and tug-of-war with sticks, staying well clear of the enormous stags who wander around like herds of four-legged hat stands.

I visit old friends whose weddings I attended 30 or more years ago. Like my brother and sister-in-law, these couples are mostly still together. I observe their relationship dynamics with David Attenborough-like fascination, imagining the natural historian's whispered voiceover in my head: *Now the male is displaying increasing irritation at his mate's attempted dominance. He feels he is in charge here, wearing the apron; he does not welcome her remark that he should either stick to the recipe or let her take over the risotto. In a moment he will issue a warning and, ah yes and there it is. The raised voice. The female looks to be retreating... but no, she responds with a joke and ... the danger is over. A quick hug, a playful flick of the tea towel, and their bond is secure.*

Because this is what I am witnessing. Not the total absence of conflict, but the ability to navigate it with humour and kindness. And to bounce quickly back to a default position of reciprocal love. No eggshell-treading. No hours of sulky silence. No desperate urge to flee the minute an inflammatory word is spoken. What are Alistair and I doing wrong? Are we simply emotionally incompatible? Did I rush towards a dream without checking its substance? Well, er, yes to the rushing part. I even joked about it. 'I barely know him. Lol.' However, I said this with the inner belief that, despite mounting evidence in my life to the contrary, love conquers all. And while it wasn't love at the start — how could it have been? — I felt sure that would come. After all, we would be living in paradise, we had similar interests, views, and a passion for all things French. Plus, our trump card — that one fundamental element that is non-negotiable and impossible to manufacture: strong mutual attraction. Chemistry? Ten out of ten.

Geography and history? A whole other story.

———————

Geography. It's one thing to be on the other side of the world from your daughters and home — and yes, New Zealand is still 'home'. But to be away from those you love so deeply AND feel lonely? I don't even know what to do with that. When Alistair and I fight, I am hollowed out. The sadness and sense of loss is out of all proportion to the disagreement itself. We have moments of happiness and incredible closeness, for sure. Yet it's transitory. It never seems to progress, to deepen. We're two lovers picnicking in the sunshine, but away in the distance the low rumble of thunder is always present.

The problem, I conclude, is that I have given up too much, travelled too far, to be with Alistair. It's as if to compensate for what I've lost, I need to gain something tremendous. It's a terrible pressure to place on a relationship, a demand of unblighted happiness. To expect it to go above and beyond, to make up for what you left behind. I know this. If Alistair and I had dated, even lived together, in New Zealand, it would have been different. But here, now, I can't stop thinking *Did I come all this way . . . for this?*

History. I can't speak for Alistair's past. That is his story to tell. But he does have wounds. I know this because he's told me, and also because only deep, deep wounds could make an emotionally intelligent, smart and otherwise loving man react to me the way he often does. He will say the same of me, just so you know.

I've mentioned my own unhappy track record in love. And it's no excuse, your honour. It doesn't give me the right to be over-sensitive and drift mournfully around the place like a wailing banshee. But it has affected me, in ways I am only just beginning to understand. Take another relationship, with Dan . . . we were living together and then suddenly we weren't.

He told me to move out. I had no money for a rental, no savings. One minute I was spooning, the next I didn't even own a fork.

So moving in with Alistair, I lived in fear of him kicking me out. There was so much at stake. Every angry look, every silence, every sigh — I saw these as entries in a ledger that would add up to 'Dear God, that woman has got to go.'

Alistair insists he was never, ever going to give me my marching orders. But that evening when he drove off, leaving me alone outside a locked *moulin*, something inside me snapped.

Which brings me onto the next gaping hole. One I should have foreseen, but didn't. The loss of a sense of self. Give me a moment here . . . this one takes a while to unfold.

That break-up with Dan back in Auckland prompted a beautiful realisation. I might be down and out, but I had a currency far more precious than any other. Friends. In that currency, I was Bill Gates. Friends came to my rescue in more ways than I can mention. Lending a van here, a sympathetic ear there. Rolling up their sleeves to help me move into a new unit. Gifting me sofas, rocking chairs, pots and pans. A colleague gave me a red wall clock she was 'only going to give to the Sally Army shop anyway' and a million items of cutlery; a long-time mate gifted me a cushion and gorgeously kitschy tray from her family bach. I received a chandelier-style lampshade that wasn't my taste but became a favourite because it sparkled like the friend who delivered it in a box. A former workmate drove over and heaved an enormous rolled-up sausage of a rug out of her boot. It was plush, designer and brand new. 'Oh I just never use it,' she said implausibly. I'd always got on fine with her . . . but I'd never have thought our friendship was of giant rug proportions. In winter, every time I went from bare floorboards to sinking my toes into that thick wool, I thought of her. Every time I would relive the break-up and start to feel rejected and unlovable, I'd look at the red clock, the rug and the blingy lampshade and be humbled into loving myself back.

It's funny. I've always been so intent on not setting store by material things that I overlooked a simple truth. That you NEED those echoes from your past, a tangible timeline of your own story.

Here in France, in the absence of family or long-standing friends, I needed more than ever to cocoon myself in memories. The problem wasn't moving onto foreign soil, but into alien domestic territory: one devoid of all reminders of who I was and where I came from.

The *moulin* is Alistair Land. Everywhere, he is in evidence. Everywhere, he is reflected back at himself. His bikes, his cars, his furniture, his TV (and unfathomable remote-control system), his habits, his photographs, his paintings, his way of cooking, his music choices. Hey, I get it. He lives here — he has every right to swaddle himself in his own comforts. So I try to embrace it. And it takes me a while to figure out why I can't. It's because when I feel sad and lost, there is no blingy lampshade to look at. When we argue, Alistair can retreat to his workshop but I have nowhere to go. Nowhere but myself, and that's often not a comforting place.

When silence moves into the space where love should be, I pull on my trainers and go running down the empty village main road, passed by the occasional tractor. The running isn't the real comfort here, the music is. Plugged into Spotify, I piece myself back together — one favourite, memory-soaked track at a time. It's an IV drip for the soul. Eventually I feel ready to return and often go and do stretches on the river bank for a few minutes, to ensure complete calm.

So yes, rather than sell every last possession when I came here, I should have brought more of those personal treasures that kept me anchored to a sense of self. I wanted to be free, unburdened by nostalgia. And now I am so unfettered I feel I might blow away.

Alistair gets frustrated when I point out that this doesn't feel like my home because there is nothing of mine here. 'But you don't own anything!' he says, in exasperation.

'But I had a car, a home, a dog!'

'You didn't own your home, your car was on finance and you could barely afford the dog,' counters Alistair.

I guess he'll never understand about the red clock and the non-matching gifted furniture.

He does have a point, though, about the money at least. And the dog. (By the way, no animals were harmed in the making of this adventure. Elio the whippet is fine and being looked after like a five-star hotel guest by my daughter and ex-husband.) But I did have independence, and the financial struggle aside, I largely felt in control.

None of this is Alistair's fault. Unless you count him exerting a pull on me that I couldn't resist. And quite honestly I am not going to complain about that. You might go your whole life without experiencing that level of magnetism, one that can draw you across an entire globe.

This is a mess of my making, not his.

I could have reduced all of the above to, 'Hey look, it just isn't working out.' But I need to put a precise lens on this. To dig deeper.

And speaking of which, it's time to talk about investigations of a different kind.

———————

The date for my MRI scan at hospital is in a week's time. That little *tache* (stain) on my chest X-ray has been largely forgotten amid climbing into windows and scanning my own emotional and spiritual wellbeing for signs of terminal damage.

I breezily tell friends, 'Ooh and guess what! I have a mark on my chest X-ray but it's probably nothing.' I don't like the way they look at me when I say this.

The test requires my return to France. I had considered trying to get it done in London, but the National Health Service is sicker than I potentially am. There is no way I will get seen quickly. Alistair insists that we put our differences aside for now, so I can come back and stay with him. At least for a while. He is worried and wants to accompany me to the hospital. I say yes because logistically it makes sense.

In truth, despite all the complications wrought by geography and history, I am missing him desperately.

———————

Alistair comes to meet me at the airport, and seeing him standing in the arrivals hall, his face full of love and concern, I feel a surge of tenderness. At first we kiss on the cheek, and do a weird awkward half-hug, but this coyness doesn't last long. It takes precisely one evening for us to be shakily back together. If the last rendition of our relationship was built on unstable ground, now we're hugging at the bottom of a landslide.

The external conditions are not promising. My visa expires in just over a month and, with that scan looming, it hasn't yet been established that I'm not about to do the same. We haven't addressed the cause of that last fight, and continuing to live in France is untenable when our relationship is in its present form. Something drastic has to change. Unless I secure more work so I can get a place of my own perhaps, or at least feel less dependent on Alistair, the prognosis for our relationship is bleak.

However, right now affairs of the heart have to play second fiddle to affairs of the lung. I need to find out what the hell is going on.

———————

The scan is worrying me for two reasons. First, the result itself. Then the cost. I don't have a *carte vitale*, or 'health card'. I have a social security number because I am paying social security contributions, but without the physical card I will have to pay for the scan upfront and claim the money back. My life support — my brother and his wife — have generously popped funds into my bank account, but I know how expensive MRIs can be. I might not have enough.

My first attempt at the scan six weeks ago failed because I was missing something vital. The procedure involves injecting you with a coloured dye, which improves image quality. I was meant to bring the dye myself — who knew? That's right, BYO meds. It's how they do things here. This time, however, I am prepared. My GP wrote me a script, the pharmacist took 56 euros, and I got a big white box full of MRI goodies. Now I arrive at the hospital proudly bearing it like I'm turning up to a party with a cake. Alistair stays in the main waiting room while my insides get their photo opportunity.

The result comes through as I am sitting by myself in a side waiting room, looking at Italian greyhound videos on my Instagram. These are the moments where life can turn on a sixpence. One minute you're looking at designer dogs and worrying the supermarket might be closed on the way home, the next understanding that mortality means you too.

The scar on my 'lung' is nothing of the sort. It's a benign tumour on my chest bone. Right now God is a middle-aged doctor in a white coat, and I want to kiss him. But I try to rein in my relief, at least until I get past the other people in that side waiting room scrolling through phones, trying to be nonchalant, awaiting their own fate.

Alistair is of course delighted. But with that worry dismissed, other concerns are up for promotion. First in line: how to pay the bill?

The admin lady looks at me sadly. '*Pas de carte vitale*?' No, but I do have my social security number, I explain brightly, and thrust it in front of her. She remains sad. 'Without the card, you must regrettably pay the full amount. I am so sorry. But you will get it back. Just keep all your receipts.' I wonder what they do in these situations if you can't pay up . . . What is the hospital equivalent of doing the washing up? Emptying bed pans?

She says a figure and I ask her to repeat it. '*Dix-neuf euros,*' she repeats. Nineteen euros. Oh France, your charms are very hard to resist!

Alistair asks, 'Shall we go for lunch to celebrate?'

It's a lovely idea, but I suggest we simply go to the supermarket. It is not yet closed.

21

Clown

Alistair's suggestion of a celebration lunch is sweet, but not really what I need. Because I know exactly what the doctor ordered in such circumstances. Three days of silliness to celebrate the joy of being alive.

And luckily, I know just where to find it.

———

It all started with the Jolie Rosette, the circus venue I described at the start of this tale. Let me refresh your memory.

Every two weeks from July, troupes of performers come to this careworn manor house near a village some twenty minutes from our home. When I say 'come', some do indeed cajole their props, pianos, wigs and paraphernalia into too-small vehicles that rattle in from out of town. Others, those who live at the manor house, simply push open the heavy front door and stroll outside onto the grassy stage of the back lawn.

All are actors, comedians, improvisers and general purveyors of madness and absurdity. And yet for me they represent a burst of sanity in an otherwise inexplicable world. It's all immensely reassuring ... their infantile curiosity, their pantomime energy, their unashamed love affair with chaos, their willingness to brazenly unzip their inhibitions and wave their imaginations around in full view of other grown-ups with mortgages, health insurance and to-do lists.

And there is a magic about La Jolie Rosette. An unreal quality. A gauzy uncertainty that lies gently over everything. Like the 'domaine mystérieuse' that is the château in the novel Le Grand Meaulnes, you almost suspect that this house and its enchanted garden might just not be there if you check the next day.

The Jolie Rosette exudes a sense of time stood still. It's a place of long grass where conspiratorial cats live and actors dream, and skinny kids run barefoot. And the world holds its breath for a night.

Everything is hints, whispers, half-truths, imaginings. Especially in the hazy light of dusk.

The entertainers are a motley line-up of jugglers, jokers, fire-eaters, comedians, buffoons, satirists and acrobats, with some having multiple talents. My favourite was a man, a clown of sorts, dressed in a white lab coat and purporting to be a nuclear scientist. After giving the audience a tour of his 'nuclear facility', he performed a spot of old-school juggling (of foam 'protons') and balanced on various 'Don't try this at home kids' items like the top bar of an easy-lift trolley. All the while he was engaged in banter with the audience and making satirical jibes about the nuclear age. He occasionally 'nuked' the children in the front row, to their utter joy, and the whole thing was dark, zany and beautiful.

Yes, I am smitten with performers and most especially clowns. I used to think they were simpletons whose idea of comedy was a shaving-cream pie in the face. No, no, and thrice no.

————————

It's not unusual to end up with a red nose after drinking to excess. In my case, a glass or three of merlot produced precisely this outcome. Except the red nose in question was fake, and attached with elastic.

You might recall that lunch at the Boutique d'à Côté, where I met clown tutor Tony? Intoxicated on wine and by the idea of a Chaplinesque version of me, I signed up for his *stage de clown* (clown workshop) to be held in September. It was a bargain 100 euros for three full days and sounded like fun.

As it turns out, the clown course couldn't be better timed. Three days after the hospital visit, and fully aware that I just dodged a bullet, I am in the mood for frivolity.

That's not to say I am free of apprehension. Apparently we all have a clown somewhere inside us, but my biggest fear is that

I won't find her (or him). That she will be buried under piles of laundry and life admin. I fear that at the closing night performance, my fellow course attendees will be bowing, patting each other on the back and taking encores and I will be laying out the after-show tea and biscuits in the kitchen.

But my brother tells me not to worry. When I suggest I will have to dig deep, he snorts. 'Your clown is right there on the surface, believe me.' This is said affectionately, though not without a dash of concern at the cavalier way I breeze through life and the chaos I leave in my wake.

On the morning of the first day, I hop into the yellow Deuche — a circus car if ever there was one — excited and nervous. I rumble in through the grand rusty iron gates of the Jolie Rosette, where some of the course attendees are staying, and meet my fellow clowns-to-be.

There is Sophie, a beautiful 26-year-old from Bordeaux whose family run a theatre company and who's been doing clown work since she could walk. Great.

There is Jerome, a 30-something with a man-bun who looks too cool for school, but who turns out to be gentle, sensitive and a great listener. I like him from our very first conversation.

Alain, in his late forties, I already know because he volunteers in the Boutique d'à Côté and is a regular at the Jolie Rosette. At the lunch where I enrolled for the clown workshop, he got up and performed a poem. For some unfathomable reason, Alain always intimidates me. Perhaps it's his intense stare and slight air of impatience.

Finally Joelle, a woman of about my age with a cascading silver bob who seems incredibly self-possessed. The sort of person who knows what to do with a pashmina and wears her maturity with confidence.

We drink an uber-fortified espresso then travel together in two cars to the community centre, our workshop venue. A large square of red carpet maps out our rehearsal and performance space, and we plonk ourselves down in a circle. Tony asks us to exchange our hopes for the course.

Sophie knows how to perform but feels her clowns are always unsubtle; she wants to work on the 'micro', the finer details of her clown persona.

Jerome has done some clown courses, absolutely loved them, and wants to learn more.

Alain describes himself as an actor interested in expanding his repertoire.

With a toss of her hair, Joelle says she's at a new chapter in her life and wants to get out of her comfort zone.

I surprise everyone and myself by launching into a mini-speech about how life is absurd, we have no control over anything, so we should just embrace and celebrate the nonsense, and clowning seems the best way to do this. They all look a little puzzled. I don't know if it's the content or the vocabulary. So I quickly add, 'And I just want to try something new.'

So that's it. Over the next three days, we return to childhood and it is the most fun and exhilarating experience of my life. Through a series of exercises, improvisations, dress-up sessions and games, we begin to breathe life into our clowns.

Jerome's clown turns out to be a Spanish man called Lorenzo el Magnifico who, when he is not looking bewildered, does everything with a flourish and a bullfighter's panache.

Sophie's is a ridiculous opera diva called Carmen who wears little black lace gloves and busts out a somewhat discordant aria at every opportunity.

Joelle's is a clumsy *femme fatale* named Michelle, who sports thigh-high boots that she caresses often. Michelle the clown has an over-inflated idea of her seductive powers.

Alain becomes Esmonde, a wild-haired buffoon in a kilt held up by braces who is easily offended.

My clown is called Maria Jesus de Los Milagros (or David for short) who trit-trots around like a pony in vertiginous pink satin heels. She also makes Tony laugh every time she opens her mouth, but I put this down to my flawed French rather than any natural theatrical talent.

So there you have it.

Several interesting points to note.

In clowning, the slightest modification to your demeanour, way of standing, where you fix your gaze — even a detail in your outfit — can change the way your character presents. Take Sophie, for instance. She has been trying overly hard to make us laugh, trilling like a soprano on meth, falling about the place and, while she's clearly confident as a performer, it all feels rather forced. But she truly steps into her Carmen persona when Tony tells her to open her eyes wide when she looks at the audience.

The effect is instant and hilarious. Her lemur-like glare and bright red-lipsticked mouth, forming an exaggerated O, make a mockery of her self-styled diva status. While elegant, beautiful and seemingly poised, the comedic expression betrays the truth. That this woman is a hot mess.

Point number two. As a wannabe clown, don't think: just act as your clown would. Thinking is your enemy. The minute you distance yourself from the character and look at it from the outside in, you lose the comedy. For the time you wear the red nose, you ARE the clown. By the way, not all clowns wear a nose but for us it's a device to signal the transition from our everyday selves to our characters. If we touch ours we have to scratch our backsides in penance. You mustn't be seen transitioning from yourself to the clown. You turn your back to the audience to *chausser le nez* (attach your nose) and turn away again to take it off.

Point number three. The art of clowning is incredibly sophisticated. And hard. To be a clown isn't simply about contrived pratfalls. It's about being entirely vulnerable and digging down into your deepest, sometimes most shameful, feelings. When you are standing there in your over-sized shoes and wonky hat, you're not just trying to make people laugh. You are aiming to connect your audience with a clown's-eye view of the world, one that's steeped in childlike curiosity and innocence. The red nose is a vehicle, a portal to a different version of us where we let go of all previous conceptions about 'how we should behave'. It's about finding the truth of a moment, and playing with that truth. Letting it breathe.

Tony describes this perfectly when he talks about *un cadeau* (a gift). For the clown, dropping your hat or accidentally breaking a chair isn't a mishap but an opportunity. It's a chance for the clown to interact with his environment and reveal another side of himself.

I receive such a *cadeau* on my clown's first solo entrance. Taking tiny goat steps in my heels to the front of the stage, I introduce myself. Silence. Tony says nothing. I say nothing. I am panicking and not sure what to do. Suddenly a fly lands on the stick I am holding upright next to my face. I glance quickly at the *mouche*, eyes swivelled towards it and wide with alarm, but still facing the audience. Tony starts to laugh. Encouraged, I take this further. I stare back at the audience, in obvious panic, then back at the fly. *'Madame, il y'a une mouche,'* says Tony. *'Oui,'* I reply. *'Une mouche. Ma mouche,'* extending the play to claim this is my pet fly that I have trained to land on the stick. It's ridiculous and impromptu, but it's causing much laughter, so I run with it. It's the most freeing thing you can possibly imagine.

The trick, of course, is not just to seize these 'gifts' but also to generate the humour and entertainment without relying on exterior provocations. It's difficult, and dispiriting when you try to be funny only to get nothing but blank faces.

But Tony is a wonderful facilitator. Even when he's not openly chuckling, he's leaning forward eagerly, a laugh just waiting in the wings, his eyes shining in anticipation and delight. Every few minutes he shouts 'PUBLIC!! (audience)' because for the clown, looking at your audience is key.

I realise this is all very 'You had to be there'. That it probably sounds infantile, pointless, not at all refined. But there is something so magical, privileged even, about being allowed to spend three days just playing. Making ourselves completely foolish, running around like idiots, being scared, joyful, trusting our clown partners to have our back on stage.

This time spent clowning is a breath of fresh air after the past few angsty months with Alistair. Our relationship has turned into a cumbersome, weighty thing — a topic of po-faced study, devoid of playfulness. When we're not engaged in open verbal warfare, we are taking faltering steps towards some form of healthy communication. And honestly? Learning to conjugate French irregular verbs was a breeze compared to this. Using non-blame, non-inflammatory 'I' statements is a noble aim. But it's hard to have a conversation that flows when you are seething with resentment *and* minding your pronouns at the same time. Saying things like, 'When you raise your voice, I feel unappreciated and unheard' is a righteous approach. But it feels constrained. Less like building bridges, more like putting traffic cones around a damaged one.

Hence the appeal of the clown's world, where making rude and silly sounds, talking gibberish and generally being immature is positively encouraged.

Each day we 'work' from 9 to 6, with an hour for lunch at a small table in the garden of the Jolie Rosette, everyone bringing a dish — home-made quiche, a courgette Thai curry with coconut sauce, goat's cheese, fresh bread, couscous salad. No wine. We want to stay focused.

On the night of the second day, we have dinner at the manor house at a large trestle table under the trees. There are light bulbs strung through the branches, it's a warm evening and Avril — one of the Jolie Rosette's resident performers — brings to the table a dish of creamy *patates dauphinoises*, spicy *merguez*, tomato and lettuce salad, crusty wholemeal bread, several bottles of red wine, a plate of cheese, and carrot cake to finish. Her five-year-old daughter Céline brings her dolls to the table and, when bored, cycles off to play with the dog, a beagle with a weakness for *camembert* and whose undercarriage sways as he pads around. I can't imagine a more dreamlike place to grow up. As I watch this carefree child clamber onto a rope swing, singing quietly to herself, I am already nostalgic on behalf of grown-up Céine. A Céline who may one day remember this place as she stares out the window of her high-rise apartment. Or not. Maybe the house will pass along to her, and the magic will continue to weave its way through her life and that of her children. I really hope so.

Around the table we chat about everything . . . including the French language, which Avril says is easier than you think. 'Forget grammar and pluperfect tenses,' she laughs. 'You just need to litter your sentences with *"bah ouai"* and *"du coup"* and you'll sound fluent!' '*Du coup*' appears to not mean anything but you hear it all the time. It's a bit like seasoning, sprinkled around sentences willy-nilly and with a value similar to 'you know' or 'like' in teen-speak.

I tell Tony I won't be able to do the next *stage de clown* if my visa isn't renewed in a couple of weeks' time. He offers to write to President Macron, or if that fails, marry me so I can stay. Everyone thinks this is a fine idea. We clink glasses and I delight in the idea of a clown wedding — complete with exploding bouquets, a bouncing wedding car and an exchange of red noses at the altar.

———————

The workshop wraps up the next day, with a very small performance to about three people, one of whom is Alistair. It's not my finest clown work, I have to admit. Even with that tiny audience, I get nervous and my clown retreats, leaving just Maria — a 64-year-old woman in a bright pink shirt with a blob of plastic on her nose. I have fallen into the trap Tony warned us about, distancing ourselves from the clown and overthinking it. But clowning takes many years to master, so I am not upset. In fact, quite the opposite. I am insanely happy. Yes, it's been exhausting and at times scary, but it's the closest I've come since arriving in France to having a true sense of belonging.

After the show we sit in our circle again, and Tony says encouraging things about our clown personas. He talks about the next course, how we'll build on what we have learned, and I so desperately want to stay for that. Though it does occur to me that deciding to stay in France should be driven by a desire to get closer to Alistair, not to a pink-heeled buffoon who exists entirely in my imagination.

We go round the hall, pulling down the blinds, rolling up the carpet, sweeping the floor, and cramming the clothes and wigs and preposterous shoes into boxes and bags. It takes just 30 minutes to dismantle the clown world and restore the real one. After ten minutes of loading, Tony's car is crammed to the gills with bright, colourful stuffing. We flop down for a cold beer at a table outside and talk — but even when the conversation has died, we sit. For a good hour we linger, as if reluctant to break the spell and return to normal life. But eventually we stand up, stretch, exchange emails and phone numbers, hug one another and say our goodbyes. We have trains to catch, places to be, water mills to drive home to.

I wander over to the 2CV and see that Alistair, who left straight after the performance, has thoughtfully rolled back the leather roof for me. I'm glad of it; it's already 7 p.m. but the sun is belting out a dazzling final number before vacating the stage. Rows of sunflowers form a rapt audience, gazing up in awe. As for me, I'm singing 'Let's Go Fly a Kite' at the top of my voice. And grinning like a fool.

22

Beauty and the Beast

We're floating in an in-between world. Happy to be reunited, sensing it can't last. We're too fiery, each of us. There are so many complex feelings — and whenever we've tried to explain and share them, we've simply pressed on each other's bruises. More triggers than a John Wayne movie (or a Quentin Tarantino film: take your generational pick).

Yet there's a tenderness here that was absent before. Over the past year we've slowly become mired in our own fears, our own pressures. Our own twisted versions of 'This *has* to work or we are lost.' Now, having actually lost one another for a while, we are overwhelmed with relief at being together again.

As the September rain pours and the river swells, as the sunbathing rock and the Jesus rock disappear beneath the fast-flowing, angry, milk-coffee-coloured current, Alistair and I begin to surface. Bobbing around, reaching out, swimming away from our respective islands. Bearing our white flags, not scrutinising each other for red ones.

Perhaps because all expectations have been suspended, we're free to breathe, to be ourselves. It's an idyllic interlude — one that feels like a honeymoon, like the start of something.

When the rains clear we head off on the e-bikes in the late afternoons — me undeterred by falling off and hurting myself badly. It's on these occasions I know that beneath Alistair's often brusque exterior, there is a kind and caring soul. When I fail to see the curve in the road, hit the kerb suddenly and go hurtling off onto hard concrete, he leaps off his bike and rushes over. My leg is throbbing (for weeks afterwards I sport a bruise like a heat map of Aotearoa on my right thigh), the skin is scraped off and blood is pouring from my palms (typical — it's the only time ever that I have not worn bike gloves), and I feel like crying. But I smile bravely. 'What an idiot!' I laugh. 'Shh,' he says gently, fussing over me, offering to go and get the car, then holding me tight like he wants to shield me from all further harm. It's this Alistair I try to hold in my mind, when doubts swirl.

———————

One unseasonably warm evening, down by the narrow penstock where the mill wheel used to churn the water, Alistair wades into the lively current in his shorts. I swelter, even in a sleeveless cotton dress, watching him with envy.

'Come in!' he urges. 'Nah' I say, but immediately contradicting myself, I lift the dress over my head, and sidle in, naked. The water is as warm as a swimming pool, and there's a smooth flat rock which nature, ever the gracious hostess, has pulled up just for me. The current eddies past and around us, bubbling here, sending up droplets there, spritzing us gently. I can't help but laugh — nothing is funny, but this carefree moment somehow demands it. For a few minutes I am not Maria with the financial worries, the homesickness, the inability to form a lasting romantic relationship, the longing for something I can't name. I am part of the river. An uncomplicated creature on a rock, basking in the elements.

As the sun warms my face, I'm reminded of *La Symphonie Pastorale*, a novel by André Gide, which I studied for French A Level. Aged seventeen, I was a little swot — or rather a *gourmande*, with an insatiable hunger for everything French. I inhaled every word and line of the compulsory texts placed in front of us. I'd never been to France but I was infatuated already and even the grim, doom-laden tales we were forced to analyse didn't put me off. *Madame Bovary, Phèdre, Thérèse Desqueyroux, La Symphonie Pastorale*. All so tragic, all so poignant to me. I blame Flaubert and Racine for making me see a certain poetry in relationship drama. I'd perhaps have been better off listening to the more prosaic dating stories of my peers, or being taught budgeting and woodwork (not available at a convent high

234

school). Heartbreak may still have found me, but at least I'd have had a financial cushion and a decent coffee table.

But back to Gide's novel, in which a married pastor adopts blind teenage orphan Gertrude. Of course she's beautiful, *de rigueur* for tragic nineteenth-century French heroines, and the pastor's handsome son has the hots for her. As does — uh-oh — the pastor. One day Gertrude regains her sight, sees the son, falls head over heels then promptly wanders out into the snow and dies. I seem to recall she sought out her own death, torn apart by the now bitter rivalry between father and son, of which she is the cause. What has all this to do with me on a rock in the river? Just that there is one passage that's always stayed with me, where sightless Gertrude, feeling the sun on her face, believes the air is singing. She confuses the birdsong and the sun's warmth as one and the same thing. '*Il lui paraissait tout naturel que l'air chaud se mît à chanter, de même que l'eau se met à bouillir près du feu.*' To her it was quite natural that the balmy air should start to produce this beautiful sound, just as water placed over a flame begins to bubble.

Funny that I should think of this now. Perhaps in this fleeting moment of simplicity and innocence, Gertrude's touching naivety somehow resonates.

———

There is no need for me to remain here. The supposed premise of my return was that urgent hospital test. But that is behind me, and the clown course too is over. (I've kept the red nose; you never know when you might need one.) I am free to go. But I am not done with this place. And maybe, just maybe, there is a chance somehow for me and Alistair.

And I've remembered that I have to be here for at least another month, to attend my French immigration department 'formation days', where I get the official introduction to French life: values, healthcare, law, geography, history, accommodation, work, education . . . the whole chipolata. Once a week for a month, these sessions are a requirement of my visa. Yes, the visa I already have. The induction was meant to take place when I first got the blessed stamp in my passport, but it has taken a while. Strictly speaking, I could skip these sessions, especially if I never intend to come back. But having formed my own opinions and prejudices about this land and its people, I'm interested to hear what France has to say about France.

My friends are concerned. They know about my swift departure to the UK, and are now justifiably asking, 'What is going on? We thought you had a big fight and it was over. Are you together or aren't you?' I have to reply, 'When I have even the faintest inkling, you will be the first to know.'

Because to be perfectly frank, I am all over the place. I am booked in for those induction sessions. I have an appointment to renew the visa and set myself on a path to that Holy Grail — French citizenship. I have all my winter clothes at my brother's house in London. Alistair and I have rekindled something, but I am not sure what. And now there is another complication.

While I was back in London — sleep-deprived, in shock, unmoored — I knew only one thing for certain: that I could never again put myself in the precarious position of relying on a man for security. My remote work had dwindled to a trickle, so I fired off job application letters north, south, east and west. For freelance jobs in London, for a full-time position in New Zealand, for work I could do remotely. I'd even wipe down café tables if it came to it. The job would decide my next move. I was casting CVs, not caution, to the wind.

When I tell Alistair that I've been on a job-hunting mission that includes the southern hemisphere, he asks (several times a day) 'If you got the role in Auckland, would you take it?' Sometimes it is said fearfully, other times sadly, and sometimes with a flicker of hostility (which I don't take offence at; I know all too well that hostility is just pain in a different costume).

For an answer, I repeat the same placeholder sentence over and over: 'Let's cross that bridge when we come to it.' This was my emotional equivalent of an 'out-of-office' email. What I really meant was, 'Please don't make me think about that right now. Let me just watch the heron. Or keep reading my book. Or watch the water rushing over the broken weir.'

I've never been good at mindfulness. But more than anything, in those moments, I wanted to live in the now.

A boyfriend once told me: 'The thing with you is you are entirely driven by your emotions.' It wasn't a criticism; more of a description. He might as well have been saying, 'You have a freckle on your shoulder' or 'You are left-handed.'

But I suspected that when it came to that bridge, Emotion and Pragmatism might be crossing it hand in hand. Because now I had to do what made sense. With no savings and no immediate income stream in sight, my financial insecurity was chipping away at an already unstable foundation. If I did get the New Zealand job, it would be a lifeline. I'd be copywriting for an agency with a strong social conscience, great values and refreshingly healthy ideas around remuneration; I would be near my daughters again, and I would be self-reliant. Safe.

As strongly drawn to one another as Alistair and I were — still are — we have hit serious problems. Because of our painful relationship histories, we trigger one another constantly. Because we can't find a way to communicate well, we create new bruises for one another rather than soothing old ones. Because we had different expectations from the outset, there is a bedrock of resentment.

Alistair: 'I thought we were going into this adventure shoulder to shoulder, the two of us taking on this new life together, facing all the obstacles side by side.'

Me: 'Hold on a minute . . . You were coming here anyway!! In fact you'd already been here for long periods of time, with Sarah. You'd already planned for this to be your permanent home when you retired; you hated New Zealand and couldn't wait to get away. So this never depended on me.'

A therapist might be shaking his or her head at this, thinking 'Oh, but all of this can be worked through. If you are both willing, you can learn to listen to each other.' It's not that we haven't considered this. We have been trying, as I mentioned, to frame things in healthier language. And Alistair has — touchingly — been absorbed of late in a book on 'relationship attachment styles' in an attempt to diagnose the problem. That man loves a manual. But somehow it all feels a little futile in the face of an ever-expanding 'Reasons for Going Back' dossier. To which I can add a new realisation: that this isn't just about me and Alistair. What about when your tumultuous love life and precarious circumstances start to hurt those you love most?

People are worrying about me. Good friends and family are no longer laughing at my 'hilarious escapades' such as hauling great ladders to climb into water mills. I'd always clung ferociously to the belief that 'You just have to live your life'. As long as you were doing no harm, I figured, you could do what you liked. But now I *am* doing harm. My volatile situation is causing concern to people who have stood by me loyally and nonjudgmentally, some of them for decades. I don't care what society at large thinks. But these people, that's different. I don't want to be their 4 a.m. worry. Of course it wouldn't matter if I could tell them, with conviction, 'No, I've got this. It's rocky right now but honestly, trust me; it's going to be fine.' But I can't tell them that. I can't tell them that because I don't believe it myself.

I have a plan B, one that won't entail me going back to New Zealand. And that is to get a well-paying freelance gig and rent a place of my own. Somewhere nearby, so Alistair and I will be close to one another. We can start afresh. We can date, and the *moulin* will return to being a *moulin* instead of a pressure cooker.

This is the only way it will work. I have convinced myself of that. Unluckily, unusually, and actually really shittily, there are no freelance gigs on the horizon.

Yet one morning, an email pings in my inbox. 'Thank you for your recent application. You are on our shortlist and we'd love to chat with you over Zoom.' It's for the Auckland role.

When Alistair asks what I plan to do, I tell him, 'Erm, well, I'm going to go ahead with the interview. I don't see that I have any alternative. I can't earn enough here to be independent.' 'Well, that's it then isn't it,' he says sadly. 'I've lost you.'

Not 100 per cent certain what our current status actually is, I sense 'lost' is not the right word. Plus I only have an interview, not the job itself. But I'm not about to start editing Alistair's sentences. It's really not the right moment for pedantry. So I say nothing. Alistair says nothing. The pause is so long, it's theatrical. For one long minute we're characters in a Harold Pinter play. Then Alistair, who has been staring out the window, suddenly turns to me. 'Let's go for a bike ride.'

It seems sensible. We can't remain standing here indefinitely, frozen and not speaking. And there's nothing like a bike ride to dispel the blues. We set off with no final destination in particular, but instinctively head towards our favourite track, the grass-covered old railway line, where Alistair slows to a halt. 'How about we go for pizza?'

The pizza place in question is some ten kilometres away, but I nod enthusiastically. On the edge of a sports field behind the *mairie* is a kiosk selling pizza and other delicious fast food, which you can eat *al fresco* at large barrels serving as tables. The larger-than-life owner has cheeks like rising dough, big meaty hands and wears a plastic headband to hold back the tide of thick grey hair. He also always seems bamboozled when we turn up and order food. The kiosk's opening hours are a little hit and miss, and it's as if he too is surprised to find himself at work behind the counter.

This evening, we arrive to find the place shuttered and deserted. Alistair looks at me apprehensively. He's studied the Maria manual and knows my settings, and is only too aware of the startlingly brief delay between 'peckish' and 'hangry'. However I simply laugh, hop back on the bike and — to Alistair's utter astonishment — whack the throttle hard.

You may remember the throttle. After several accidents, Alistair has repositioned this perilous device to a safer place on the handlebars (where I can't trigger it by accident), but until today I have steadfastly refused to use it. Now I go blurring past him, yelling, 'Let's go to Philippe's!'. Chez Philippe, a restaurant, is a 25-minute ride back to home, but the very thought of food is enough to jet-propel me through the evening air.

Some twenty minutes later we screech to a halt outside Philippe's, where I promptly order a Kir and a large chicken burger with extra fries. 'Who are you and what have you done with Maria?' says Alistair admiringly.

We drink a few *rosés* too many, forget our hats and sunnies on the table, and teeter off into the setting sun, startling cows and batting away midges as we go. Back home, Alistair hits Spotify and cranks the music up loud. The sound blasts from two colossal speakers; Alistair is immensely proud of these wooden megaliths he built himself, fondly dubbing them 'Stonehenge'. We dance like demons to James Brown, then slow-waltz to Dionne Warwick and Fleetwood Mac and there's more cheese here than in all the pizza food trucks in all the world, but I don't care. I nuzzle into Alistair, and he squeezes me tighter, and right now there are no job interviews, no sadness or goodbyes. Just me, him, and a 200-year-old *moulin* turned boombox for the night.

———

So when an adventure turns into *un bordel* (a mess), what is the best way forward? Toss a coin? Make an Excel spreadsheet? Draw up lists? Get therapy? Meditate? *Mais non.* The answer is: go on another adventure.

It's Alistair's idea.

'I want us to explore more of France together. Whether you stay or go; I want to give this to you.'

I am definitely up for it. At least I am up for it in its initial guise — a camping trip. Low-key, pootling around in the Berlingo, eating beans on a campfire, snuggling up and looking at the stars.

Then the plan undergoes a radical makeover.

'How about . . .' begins Alistair, in an overly eager tone that puts me on alert.

'Okay, I said camping,' he continues. 'But . . .' His eyes are shining and his buoyant enthusiasm is verging on pantomime.

I half expect him to slap his thigh and burst into song.

'. . . how about we go on the bike!!'

And there it is. The staff in my alarm-bells department are high-fiving each other at being on the money. 'The bike' means the motorbike, aka The Beast (which is what aficionados fondly call the brutish KTM model). Yes, I have to some extent overcome my fears, but only when it comes to brief stints on the pillion and breezing along country lanes. A three- to four-day motorbike tour on fast, busy roads is a whole other kettle of *poisson*.

Before I can say anything, Alistair is off again.

'So, we go on the bike. Obviously we'll have to pack light but we can stay in hotels along the way. We'll just set off and see what takes our fancy!'

The word 'hotels' has acted like a warm, soothing facecloth on my apprehensions.

'Go on,' I reply.

'So I promise to not ride like a lunatic; you will be comfy because it's the bigger bike and it will be an adventure! On the bike, you'll see, it's totally different. You get to really experience the countryside, smell the smells. You are *immersed*. It's a whole different view. No bits of car window in your way. Just you and nature.'

And the tarmac. And a herd of crazy drivers. And the possibility of English tourists coming at us on the wrong side of the road (this happened to a UK friend of ours recently. Drove on the left, swerved to avoid an oncoming car, then smashed into a tree. Thankfully, both drivers are fine. '*Ah, les anglais*!' said a French friend when we told him. 'They always do this!' he added, like it was a favourite British pastime.)

But Alistair's boyish zeal is endearing, and I trust him to keep us safe. He does love speed, but he also knows what to look out for, how to avoid the nutters, mitigate the dangers. He did an advanced motorbike course with the cops and, say what you will about the police, you don't hear of them falling off bikes very often.

So it's settled. I pack very light (which I am to regret) and a tad impractically: a pair of shorts; two tops; the big, baggy, black denim biker pants with lining; three pairs of socks; five pairs of earrings; a swimsuit; three pairs of undies; my Kindle; some shortbread; mascara and lipstick; a toothbrush; and a tiny little metallic guardian angel that my brother and Fiona gave me when I left London.

Panniers packed, *moulin* locked, helmets and gloves on, we set off. Bound for Périgord, as the French know it. Or what property-eyeing Brits fondly call the Dordogne.

———————

Alistair didn't over-sell it. A motorbike road trip is amazing. At first I clutch him hard around the waist, like it's *his* life I am trying to save. Then gradually I relax, sometimes even letting go and just holding the side handles to steady myself.

I get to feel the rhythm, the patterns of Alistair's acceleration, to anticipate the G-force. The first time he overtakes two trucks, he taps my leg to warn me and we roar into the atmosphere. I lean in and grab him tighter, a needy koala. But I soon understand Alistair's strategy, observe that he never overtakes anywhere near a bend or a hill, that even on the straight he won't pull out unless the road is clear a long way ahead. Plus on a bike that does 0 to 200 kilometres in 7.2 seconds (a bit like my hunger), you're always going to leave the trucks standing.

I start to detect patterns. When there are sluggish cars up in front, Alistair edges up behind them, moving out slightly to indicate his intention to overtake at the next possible opportunity. The French, as it turns out, are very respectful of bikers; almost without exception they veer to the side to make room. The minute any oncoming cars have passed, the bike screams into action and for a few seconds we are almost airborne. Alistair once met a test-pilot for fighter planes who told him the next best thing to the exhilaration of flying was riding a motorbike. I can believe it.

The journey takes us through ever-prettier hamlets with weathered walls and mediaeval *châteaux* on the horizon. History unfurls alongside us — the bike clocking up centuries, not just kilometres, as we go.

We bump over the cobbles of the first village, thrumming along so slowly now that we can smell the sweet, oily fragrance of what may be *beignets* (doughnuts) or perhaps *crêpes* wafting from an open window. The low growl of the engine is the only sound, except for a sudden 'wow' from a teenage girl out for a morning walk with her *copines*.

Then we're off again, out on the open road. The scenery whooshes past us, a crazy kaleidoscope of images: a piebald foal; grass so vividly lime-green it might have been drawn with marker; swathes of shrivelled sunflowers, their scrunched-up heads like a vast tray of golden popcorn; an unshaven chin of a field, all stubble and sharp stalks. At times we're screaming along so fast, we're a chainsaw tearing its way through botanical-patterned fabric.

In Thiviers, finally in the Dordogne, we stop for a *tarte aux framboises* — a delicious golden, crusty pastry base and creamy custard piled high with raspberries. We sit outside a *tabac*, on a pavement so narrow our chairs are almost on the road, and take in the view. The French strictness about mealtimes means that between breakfast and lunch, not many places serve food at all. It's quite acceptable to order a cognac or a Ricard and water, but ask for a sandwich and they look at you quizzically. It's perfectly okay, however, to visit the *boulangerie* and bring your sandwich or fruit tart back to the café to enjoy with your coffee or morning snifter.

Our next stop is Bergerac, which apparently has a lovely old quarter with picturesque squares. I say 'apparently' because our experience includes none of this. We stay at a 'games-themed' hotel a little outside of town — a huge modern complex with a swimming pool and whose unique selling point is a massive supply of board games and even an escape room, where you get a series of clues to help you find your way out. Looking back later, that is my main memory of Bergerac. That and the long walk into town on a stifling hot night, incredible for the time of year, in my thick biker pants and with hair spiralling in all directions — having swum in the pool and forgotten my straighteners. Alistair is delighted, he loves my curls and pats them constantly. I'm not a fan. My head feels messy enough on the inside, without this external chaos.

We spy an attractive restaurant right by the river, with a huge terrace and only one table occupied. But when we tell the *maître d'* we'd like to eat, she somewhat haughtily asks if we've booked. We haven't, but gesture to the empty terrace. 'Ah but no, I regret you cannot if you have not reserved,' she replies, her cool tone and overly sweet smile suggesting victory rather than regret. On leaving we notice the restaurant's three Michelin stars, and I speculate that one of them might reside up the *maître d'*'s rear.

The snub turns out to be a blessing: as we wander around in search of a more welcoming place to eat, we spot an unassuming Portuguese bistro squeezed in beside an ugly, windowless masonic church facing a small square. There are three small metal tables outside, teetering on the edge of a cobbled car park. A Portuguese woman with a large girth and a wide smile gestures to one of the tables. She carries her own Mediterranean micro-climate, exuding warmth and *bonhomie*, in sharp contrast to the Arctic chill of the previous establishment. We sit *al fresco*, drinking *rosé* and eating *bacalao* (cod) *croquettes* followed by pork chops and more cod with potatoes, our table lit up alternately by a tiny flickering candle and the rear lights of vehicles reversing perilously close to our chairs.

As we sit in the sultry storm-gathering night, Alistair points out the Périgord-style roofs all around the square: steep-pitched with a tiny outward flick at the bottom. These particular examples are like a mouth of wonky teeth, all crooked and at different heights.

To outsiders, we must appear like one of those blessed couples that the years have drawn ever closer. A small curly-haired woman in too-big pants, and a silver-goateed bear of a man laughing, chatting and holding hands across the table. Time may be running out for us, but we are steadfastly committed to this moment, to this version of us. Like method actors unable — or even afraid — to step out of character.

———

The following day we check out of the games hotel, and point the bike eastwards in the direction of the Château de Castelnaud, some 60 kilometres away.

Alistair has long wanted to visit this castle, and at first it's hard to see why. Arriving at the rather desolate car park we lock the panniers to protect our valuables (actually I have none, unless you count the shortbread, my notebooks and a favourite pair of earrings) then follow the signs up to the *château*. And now I get it. First we come upon Castelnaud-la-Chapelle: the most sublimes of villages, it is pure *Beauty and the Beast* territory. Narrow, windy streets; biscuit-coloured stone houses, some half-timbered; those unmistakable roofs; ancient stone arches . . . I half expect to see Belle and Gaston, and villagers throwing open their wooden shutters with a merry chorus of *'Bonjour, bonjour!!'*

The castle is incredible; it has stood watch for some eight centuries high above the Dordogne river — brooding, tense and ever ready for attack. It changed hands seven times between the French and the English during the Hundred Years' War. That was property acquisition in the late Middle Ages, so actually let's not be mean about estate agents. The English invasion continues apace, of course, with some 7000 Brits now living in the Dordogne.

When I think of that castle later, I recall never-ending flights of stone steps, the medieval armour and savage weaponry on display — the terrible lances, terrifying crossbows and other paraphernalia of violence all at peace now in their glass cabinets. I remember the spectacular view from the ramparts, looking down on the river — the canoes slow-moving specks far below — and Beynac Castle perched high on a distant cliff. But what I recall most is a rather peculiar occurrence.

We have just made our way to the first part of the fortress tour, a throne room with mannequins wearing rough woollen tunics and itchy-looking tights. I turn to joke to Alistair about the 'man bag' slung from the belt of one young plastic prince, but he is not there. Not worried by the fact that he's continued without me, I proceed to the next chamber. In a darkened room, a few tourists are hunched over an illuminated miniature model of the castle and surroundings. No sign of Alistair. I enter the next room, and the next, and I am hurrying now. How did he manage to evaporate entirely?

Everywhere people are lingering; there's a lot to see. In a scullery a giant stuffed boar is slung from the ceiling, and what looks like a bathtub sits improbably in one corner. In another room are more deadly spiked weapons; in the next a video plays, a sombre-voiced narrator relaying the fortress's dark history. I give these things no more than a passing glance. More staircases, winding round and down, then snaking back up again. I emerge into the open air onto the ramparts again and lean over the thick stone to scan the courtyard far below. Scurrying back along the rampart, I'm chased by a sense of foreboding. Down the steps, through an arch. The end of the tour. Alistair has vanished. And here's the peculiar thing. Like a four-year-old lost in a mall, I feel a lump in my throat and the tears hot behind my eyes. *Ridiculous woman*, I half-laugh to myself but no, there it is, I am crying. Alistair isn't there, and this sense of loss is way out of proportion. It's beyond all reason. It simply makes no sense. My phone battery is dead but I know where the bike is, I know he is here somewhere, we will meet up in a moment. And the setting — with its centuries of bloodshed, battle and true heartache — makes this mini-drama all the more absurd.

In some desolate dungeon of my mind, a thought, a realisation is locked away. It can't reach me, but it has sent messengers. A racing heart, a hollow sensation, the tears still streaming. Some part of me knows something that I, the present me, only half-senses.

I retrace my steps, take one last look down into the courtyard and, finally, there he is. I yell, my voice thin and feathery across the distance, but he glances up and we both laugh. I run down to meet him, he rushes towards me. And this is the strangest part of all. Alistair wraps me in the biggest hug and whispers, 'You know it's stupid, but I had separation anxiety. I felt like crying. Ridiculous, eh?' 'Utterly pathetic,' I reply and quickly wipe away a tear.

———

Things I've learned about biking.

When it's unbearably hot, you take off your T-shirt, soak it in cold water in the nearest loos / fountain / river, and pop it back on to wear under your biker gear. We do this in public toilets at the castle. It is heaven, and walking to the bike in a sodden T-shirt amid hordes of well-turned-out tourists feels beautifully improper.

You must put on your wet-weather gear at the very first hint of rain. I don't — and spend 40 minutes on the way home with the cold rivulets trickling down my back, shivering and convinced I am developing hypothermia.

When you see another biker passing you, hold two fingers out to the side — in a peace sign yet down low, at hip height. It's a biker brethren thing, and I love it. Passengers can also get in on the act. Pillions are people too.

What can I tell you about the next few days? That they are an interlude, an illusion . . . a momentary escape where nothing real or meaningful takes place? Or that they are the closest that Alistair and I have ever felt, the most clearly we have understood each other?

I can tell you how he laughs when I buy a hemp hat to hide my curls, and kisses the top of my head when I remove it momentarily. How we drink just-sweet-enough homemade lemonade at the Château des Milandes, home for 30 years to the legendary dancer and political heroine, Joséphine Baker, a black civil-rights activist and mother to twelve adopted children.

I can describe the heavy, brooding night that we eat on the upstairs balcony of a restaurant tucked down an alleyway in Sarlat, Alistair insisting we remain *al fresco* despite hard drops of rain that I know have every intention of growing up to be a deluge. Of him mocking me as I retreat, the electric storm lighting up a suit of armour hanging above the restaurant entrance, and the downpour filling every wine glass with water within seconds. Of the delicious, butter-soft trout (which, had we stayed on the balcony, would have posthumously swum away on a river of rainwater).

I can tell you about the dog we encounter in the little bar opposite our hotel, an adorable teddy bear of a thing with giant paws and a great floppy fringe which almost takes Alistair's hand off when he tries to pat it through the wooden gate that separates it from the clientele. We learn that the dog — property and wingman of the bar owner — has exactly twenty friends (all human) and he chooses them carefully. 'How long does it take for him to befriend you?' I ask, wanting desperately to be part of this inner circle. '*Bah, c'est lui qui décide*,' replies the large, bearded, Hagrid-esque owner. 'It's up to him. You may never make it.'

Above all, I can tell you of the bonding power of being on that bike. Maybe it's the enforced hugging, the knife-edge sense of never feeling more alive or so close to death, the gratitude to Alistair for keeping us safe, the sense of us being two explorers propelled through time and space. Together.

We arrive home, bike-sore, wet and thoroughly content.

Two days later I open my email to find I've landed the job in New Zealand.

23

A Romantic and
a Belated Pragmatist

From the moment I receive the job offer, Alistair is not happy. In fact that is an understatement. For several days afterwards, I wake at night to find the space next to me empty and Alistair downstairs, either on his phone or with a glass of wine. The lack of sleep doesn't help him to temper his emotions. He veers wildly between anger at me and inconsolable sadness. And it is breaking my heart.

––––––––––

For the past few weeks, I have been attending further 'induction' days as required by my visa conditions. Since I've been in limbo

— not knowing whether or not to extend my *carte de séjour* —
I have been turning up to these sessions just in case.

The instruction has been highly informative, and entertaining. Our *formatrice* (instructor) for the first two weeks is a wonderful woman called Nicole, who is extremely jolly and jokey. She talks us through all the different ways France is carved up — regions, departments and communes — then the principles on which the country is founded. She shows us the four symbols of the *République*: the *tricolore* (French flag); the 'Marseillaise' (the national anthem); Marianne (a fictional character, shown wearing a revolutionary bonnet); and finally *le coq* (the rooster). Nicole asks 'Does anyone know why the rooster?' 'Ooh-ooh,' I say, with Hermione Granger-like eagerness. 'Because the revolution was the dawn of a new day!' Nicole looks over her glasses and smiles. '*C'est très jolie, mais non*!' (that's very pretty, but no). The explanation, far duller than mine, is that under the Romans, France was called Gaulle, and 'gallus' in Latin means cockerel.

Nicole makes the sessions fun and interactive, and I warm to her further when one afternoon, she looks around her room full of immigrants. We are a mixed bunch: me (English, Kiwi, South American), Moroccan, African, Japanese, Algerian, Turkish. After surveying us all, she launches into a monologue about the role of immigration in France. She talks about Senegalese-born poet and writer Léopold Sédar Senghor, who fought in the French army, was imprisoned by the Germans and went on to become president of Senegal. 'He has a street named after him, right here!' she says animatedly. She tells us about an immigrant in Grenoble who is testing an anti-cancer vaccine. She doesn't say it outright, but her impromptu speech has 'You are so welcome here' written all over it.

One lunchtime, she taps me on the shoulder. 'Would you be interested in translating, at days like these?' she asks. Hugely flattered, I say 'Well, yes.' The sessions are all in French and some attendees have translators murmuring quietly at their elbow. A translating role appeals enormously. Not only would it be much-needed income, but I'd be helping people to integrate. People who, as I've already mentioned, might be here not to follow a dream but to escape a nightmare.

On the third induction day, Nicole is replaced by a far more severe tutor who insists on being addressed as Monsieur G, won't let us drink coffee, then bangs the desk of one student who is nodding off to sleep in the stuffy room. But he's extremely knowl-edgeable and over just three hours rattles through all the high points of French history. Not for the first time, I feel honoured to even be temporarily living in a country with a history as rich as this. Yes, that past includes colonialism and present-day France has its ugly sides, not least the rise of Le Pen and the far right. But to be able to lay claim to a proud revolutionary tradition, to me that is still quite something.

————————

Yet what of me and Alistair? What about the man I truly believed was finally my chance at lasting love?

The problem was we became infatuated quickly. I say 'infatuated', because how can you love someone when you don't know them? If we did fall in love, it was with the idea of us. With our whole unwritten story. If we were ever shoulder to shoulder in anything, it was in our unspoken mission. To prove to the world that age is no barrier to passion and adventure (I still believe that, by the way). And our remedy to the shortest dating period ever? A 'boots and all' approach: We will MAKE it work by being in a situation where the stakes are too high for it not to. Was that love or lunacy — and are they really that different?

If I did fall in love with Alistair, I honestly can't pinpoint when I fell out of it. Is falling out of love the work of a moment — a piece of vulnerability, a look, a comment, a tone that suddenly rings false? Is it an accumulation of all of the above, bubbling away over time? Or is it that you fall out of love with who *you* are when you are around him/her/them?

So many questions. Yet one thing I know for sure is that if I leave, I will miss Alistair intensely. How could I not, when we have been together so constantly for well over a year? When everything falls into place, when our moods chime and all is going well, we revel in each other's company. We can talk for hours (though we still don't laugh enough). I also have a huge level of admiration for him. For holding tight to his dream — for seeing the beauty and magic in an old mill that many would dismiss as too cold, too impractical, too down-at-heel. The mill was never meant to be lived in, and even after it was converted into accommodation status it was pretty rough and ready. Alistair has had to work hard — mentally and physically — to outwit the constant winter draughts, keep the flooding at bay when the river pours over the banks, do battle with obstinate utility companies to ensure a steady gas supply, wage war on the overgrown gardens, and a myriad of other challenges that would have broken a lesser man. Or that would have had many 60-something men reaching for the 'lock and leave' property brochures. But he's stoic. And he's a romantic. His passion for the river, for the sheer poetry of the place . . . perhaps that's what I fell in love with. His lyrical Irish spirit.

Alistair wanted me to be the love of his life. But I believe the mill can probably lay claim to that. I no longer want to be part of destroying whatever magic they have between them. I want him to find his paradise again.

———————

It makes practical sense to leave, to resume my life in Auckland. But — and pardon me if I quote myself here — 'Just because something makes sense doesn't make it easy.' That is what I said at the start of this tale, and it holds true now.

It's a cruel irony that just as you are mentally preparing to leave a place, it starts to embrace you. It begins to reveal its deeper self, it takes your hand and says gently: 'Must you really go?'

Maybe this is where I have also gone wrong — thinking it was all down to me, that settling in was something I could plan for and make happen. Yes, you can play a part, and I have. You can polish your French grammar, you can smile like a fiend at every single person you meet, say 'yes' and 'yes' and 'yes' again. Ultimately though, it's really a matter of time. There is a point at which the place comes to *you*.

And so it is that after the job offer, I find myself having longer conversations with Annette, owner of the minimart off the square. We've always smiled and nodded and exchanged niceties, but we're slowly moving on from that. She is warm and always interested in what you have to say; her eagerness to chat is genuine. I feel she is someone I could befriend.

In the hairdresser (where they charge a mere 60 euros for full colour, treatment, cut and *le brushing* — blow-dry), I bump into our lovely Norwegian friend, and we sit and talk for hours. I am cheating age with a root touch-up while she is making peace with it, letting her thick hair return to grey. Sipping our tea and chattering away under our foils, it feels cosy and familiar. It feels like fitting in.

Then in the Boutique d'à Côté one morning, I see a figure crouched down, sweeping up some broken glass with a dustpan and brush. Realising it is Alain — who volunteers in the shop and was on the clown course with me — I tap him on the shoulder and say his clown name. 'Esmonde!' Before the course, Alain and I never had much to say to one another. Now however he leaps up and there is genuine delight in his eyes as he goes in for an enthusiastic hug. There is something about this encounter that is deeply moving. Even Alistair comments on it. 'Wow, he really was happy to see you!'

At the counter with our bulging basket of veges, cheese, meat and eggs, we realise we don't have money for the 48 euro bill. We have bank cards, but in smaller shops and even hairdressers, it's common for them to accept only *espèces* (cash) and cheque. 'So sorry,' we tell Madame D, one half of the couple who run the place and who is working on the till. 'Would you mind keeping our bags while we race to the ATM?' On our return we ask, 'It was 48 euros, wasn't it?' 'No,' says Madame D gravely. 'Now it's 52.' Then she laughs, and we laugh, and are flattered at the gentle mockery that comes from familiarity.

Silly little moments that say in a big voice '*Now* you are starting to belong.'

Am I really able to leave all of this? Am I really ready to go?

24

Belonging

White birds fly low over the water, some just skimming the surface. It's a sunny, slightly hazy November morning.

'It's so beautiful here,' says Alistair. 'I know it won't last, but right now it's magical.'

'It's always magical,' I reply. 'Even in deepest winter. Just in a chillier, bleaker way.'

I close my eyes for a second and breathe deeply, as if trying to inhale the magic — to take the village, the *moulin*, the river into my lungs.

I look back at Alistair. 'Oh, I meant to tell you. Do you remember Eleanor, the English woman we met at the *fête*? You know the one — funny teeth, talks fast, really friendly. And her partner Robin, Robert . . . anyway, so weird but she texted me yesterday, to say they're back in Nérignac and invited us to dinner! After all this time.'

'And are we going?' asks Alistair, with the faintest smile.

'Yeah, why not?'

'No really, what did you say?'

'I said we were co-writing a book on relationships and were way too busy right now.'

'Not funny.'

'Actually, I haven't replied yet.'

We talk a little more, then I press the red 'end call' button and Alistair vanishes. Along with the French trees and the French moon and the iridescent French sky. All of it gone.

It doesn't matter, though, that my phone has swallowed the scene. Every last detail is etched into my memory. The rock in the middle of the river with a tiny tuft of grass on top that sticks up like those ridiculous ponytails you see on babies. The way the water pours pink and orange over the weir at sunset. The dark silhouette of the barns and houses in the distance, mostly concealed by trees. And if you lean out just a little, you might see Jacqueline on her knees weeding, or Gabriel pulling the kayak out for an evening trip down the river.

As for Alistair, I can't just see him; I can feel him. His arm around my shoulders, his solid presence.

There was talk of us coming back to New Zealand together, and in many ways I am glad Alistair didn't return with me. Why should he leave a place so close to his heart so that I can be in the one closest to mine? I so badly wanted to write a love story.

And in a way I have, just not the one I intended. Because if love is belonging, a deep knowing that you are home, I have finally found it. Or rather, recognised it for what it is.

The dog scampers up and drops his frisbee hopefully at my feet — he doesn't like to be ignored. I scratch him under the chin, spin the red plastic disc through the air, then look back at the ocean. Ah yes, the River Vienne is so beautiful. But the Hauraki Gulf, spread before me, is beautiful too. And at a certain point she blends with the horizon, so you can't be quite sure where she begins and ends. Just like a dream.

Acknowledgements

Throughout this whole adventure, so many wonderful people had my back. Family, friends and workmates made me feel that it would all be okay, that I was okay, that I had a safe harbour to return to if things went wrong. They didn't judge, they didn't lecture — they waved me off with such generosity and goodwill I felt exceptionally humbled. I will forget to mention some of these fantastic individuals, no doubt, but here goes:

My former workmates Leigh, Cherise, Chelsea, Cess and Nadine. Despite me leaving the full-time role after just six months because a man waved his water-mill photos at me, they couldn't have been more accommodating. (Special shoutout to Cess and Nadine, for urging me to write. Nadine, your feedback on those early chapters was so valuable).

My ex-hubby Lindsay, for taking the dog and daughter to live with him when I left for France. There was initially some understandable grumbling. About the dog, that is; the daughter can take herself for walks. Two years on, he and the whippet are inseparable.

Mary, she of the Venice jigsaw. She listened, read, expressed delight and encouragement at my initial efforts, gently suggested and edited, and was there whenever I felt lost and homesick. It never ceased to amaze me how she always, always picked up the phone. All of this despite the fact we had floated the idea of going to Europe together. I ditched her for a man and she hasn't just forgiven me; she has been one of my biggest supporters.

Becky, a piece of scaffolding in human form who has stopped me from collapsing in on myself more times than I can count. Her 'how to be a friend' philosophy should be part of the national curriculum.

Ditto for Erica and Bill — who made their home my home while I was in the UK. After some five days of wining and dining me like an empress and not letting me pay for a thing, Erica said 'Do come back any time' and didn't flinch when I returned about a week later. She fuelled my creativity with cups of tea and biscuits and was unselfish to the core. Nicky, the true friend she's always been, also said I had a home with her if my French adventure imploded. The amazing Tricia and Clive, whose company was a miracle tonic during a particularly hard episode, despite having their own grief to contend with. That's what almost five decades of friendship will do.

Liz and Howard — thank you for your kindness; you are the best. Side note: my mission was actually redundant; you had already proved that love is possible at any age. Philippa for being a champion listener. Kate for standing by me despite having known me so briefly.

Eleanor Black for her encouragement, sage advice and generosity with her knowledge and time. Michelle, Leonie and the team at Allen & Unwin for placing their trust in me, and being amazing to deal with every step of the way. Emma, who edited my ramblings with so much intelligence, delicacy and wisdom. Sophie, the illustrator, for creating a cover that beautifully captures the spirit in which I embarked on this whole affair.

My dear longtime friend Joanna for always, always believing in me and being the sister I never had. You told me you'd drive to France to get me if I said the word, and I know you absolutely would have.

My French friends and neighbours. *Merci* for all the *apéros* and kindness.

William and Fiona (and Colin). You are and always have been my guardian angels. The knowledge of 'Ma's upstairs room' galvanised me no end. You are the kindest and best people I know. And Guinness (RIP) — you were the cutest kind of therapy, my little friend.

Last but so not least. My daughters. It was you, not the watermill photos, that set me off on this adventure. I wanted to show you that life doesn't have to follow anyone's trajectory but the one you choose. That a little madness is key. Still, I worried you'd see it as selfish. But your generosity of spirit blew me away. You are my constant inspiration and joy, and I love you all the way to France. And back.